Learning Thai, Your Great Adventure

by Russ Crowley & Duangta Wanthong Mondi

Published by Russ Crowley

Learning Thai, Your Great Adventure

www.ltyga.com

Copyright © 2011 by Russ Crowley

ISBN 978-1-908203-00-7 (pbk)
ISBN 978-1-908203-01-4 (ebk)

Front cover and all illustrations by Toni Howard.

Tone graph created and drawn by Russ Crowley.

All photographs by Russ Crowley.

Translated by Duangta Wanthong Mondi.

For Joan and Bill Crowley, mum & dad.

Table of Contents

Consonant Story   45

Introduction

I have a number of Thai language books in my reference library and they provide most of the information I need but, unfortunately, they don't cover all of my requirements.

It is with this aim in mind that I decided to write this book. It is the kind of book that if I was starting afresh, I would want at the top of my study pile.

It will be used as the first book on your path to learning to speak, read, and write Thai language. In easy to follow steps, it will guide you through learning the letters of the alphabet, to reading, speaking, writing and understanding Thai.

It will provide a readily available quick reference to the Thai alphabet: its characteristics, sounds, shapes and pronunciation; it will help you to recognise the individual words in Thai script and to assist you in 'breaking down' and identifying the words in a sentence.

Its convenient size means you can slide it in alongside your laptop, your gym kit or your shopping bag and refer to it when you get a few minutes to spare waiting for the train or the bus. It has been designed so

Wat Sothonwararam Worawihan, 'Wat Hong',
Chachoengsao Province.

you don't have to look far for information and will, of course, always be available as an aide-memoir to be referred to as your proficiency improves.

Who is this Book For

This book is aimed at anyone who wants to learn to speak, read and write Thai language.

It will be of great use to the first time holidaymaker, the seasoned traveller or for anyone who wants to spend more time in the Land of Smiles (LOS) and wants to improve their level of Thai. From the novice through to the experienced, this book is for you.

This book will not get you to an advanced level of Thai, that would require one many times this size. It will, however, get you started and quickly help you achieve a basic level of speaking, reading and writing Thai. This will then provide a solid platform for continuation of your Thai language studies.

How to Use this Book

When learning any language there is a lot to initially digest and Thai is no exception. The language is new, the alphabet and written characters are unlike anything you've seen before and, at first glance, there are few similarities.

There is a lot of information to digest in this book but it would be almost impossible to expect you to do this at your first attempt. The key to effective learning is little and often.

Wat Pra Sing Waramahawihan, Chiang Mai

If you wish to get started with Thai phrases then you can either go to the first page of the story (the *Chicken*, page 46) and read and learn from the transliterated Thai and the English translation of common sentences, or you can go to *Useful Phrases* in Appendix F, page 153.

However, if you do wish to learn the alphabet and how to read and write Thai then you have to learn the consonants first, it has to be done, there is no way around this.

In Thai, consonants and vowels have to be learnt separately as they can not be combined into an easy method such as the Roman alphabets' A, B, C... Begin by learning the consonants with the yellow header and footer bar, these are called the *Middle Class* consonants.

The Middle Class is the best place to start as there are only 9 consonants. Learn the shapes, their meaning, their tone and their consonant sound(s). On all of the pages you will see words, sentences and information to help you improve your language ability.

Everybody has specific ways they like to learn and it is up to you to determine yours. Whatever method you use, remember that when learning any language, regular sessions are necessary and immersing yourself and practising at any opportunity will reap dividends.

Of course, if you only visit the LOS on holiday then this may be a little difficult. However, there is now a wealth of information available on the Internet to help: websites, podcasts, chat, etc. There are always *genuine* Thai people who would love to converse with you. This way you can practice your Thai and they can practice their English.

When you combine the information from this book with actually using Thai, your time in Thailand will be further enriched by having made new friends on the way.

The Thai Alphabet

1. The Alphabet

There are 44 consonants (อัก-ษร - àk-sɔ̌ɔn,[1] *consonant*) in the Thai language and 32 vowels (ส-ระ - sà-rà, *vowel*). Vowels are placed in front of, above, below and behind consonants; there are other strange marks written above the consonants and the vowels and all of these are brand new to you! Don't worry, all will be explained in this book.

One of the main differences between the English and Thai languages is that Thai is a tonal language. It is important that you get the tone correct: if you don't, there may be occasions when it may be difficult to get your message across.

Transliterated Thai

As a beginner, I can assure you that you are not alone in the thought that Thai script appears almost unintelligible: there is no similarity between the Roman and Thai alphabets and the assumption, for a lot of people, is it's too difficult or they just don't have the time.

Don't be put off by this. You wouldn't have bought this book if you didn't want to learn. Granted, the initial learning curve is fairly steep but it gets easier once you have grasped the basics.

Of course, we are learning a whole new system and until you have picked up the basics, we'll use a transliterated text throughout this book.

Transliterated Thai is a romanised translation of Thai script and incorporates syllable breakdown and correct tone. Unfortunately, there is no agreed transliteration of Thai script and it is quite possible to pick up three or four books on learning Thai and find three or four different transliteration systems.

This difference means you are effectively learning a useless language instead of learning Thai script and, ultimately, you are wasting your own time. I cannot emphasise enough the need to start learning Thai script from the outset. Initially it may be difficult but once you have the basics, you'll be so pleased that you did.

In my experience, the most accurate and easiest transliterated system to use is that developed by Paiboon Publishing.

It is a simple to use, comprehensive system that incorporates the information you need to understand and speak Thai. There are a number of benefits of

---

[1] Don't worry about how to pronounce this at the moment, all will be revealed soon.

their system, one of which is in the use of a single letter to represent short vowels and a double letter for long vowels: it is simple, obvious and provides an easy-to-see and easy-to-use method of differentiating between similar words. They have kindly granted permission for us to use their Paiboon and Paiboon+ systems and we will be using them throughout this book.

Writing Transliterated Tones

There are 5 tones in Thai (high, mid, low, falling and rising) and, when we write transliterated text, we write the tone mark above the first vowel in the word as shown in Table 1.1. The table also shows examples of how the tones are written and how the tone is to be pronounced.

With each tone it is important that you understand the level where the tone starts, this is key! For example, low tone may sound similar to falling tone at first but remember that low tone *starts* below mid tone and keeps dropping, whereas falling tone *starts* higher than mid tone and then it drops [below your mid tone].

Table 1.1 - Transliterated Thai Tone Marks

Tone	Tone Mark	Transliterated Thai Example	You Say it With…
Middle	No tone sign	Gaa	…your normal voice, constant pitch.
Low	\	Gàa	…your voice *starting* at a slightly lower pitch than your normal (mid tone) voice and dropping throughout.
Falling	^	Gâa	…your voice *starting* higher than your mid tone and finishing lower than mid tone.
High	/	Gáa	…your voice *starting* higher than mid tone and rising throughout.
Rising	v	Gǎa	…your voice *starting* slightly lower than mid tone and finishing high.

Note: The symbols used to identify tone are *only used in transliterated script*. Thai script has its own written tone marks, these are covered in section 5.

Why are there two aa's in the above table? As we mentioned above, the transliteration system uses single vowels to represent short Thai vowels and a double vowel to represent long Thai vowels.

Every Thai student learns the **base** tone sequence for Middle Class conso-nants: *gaa, gàa, gâa, gáa, gǎa* - *middle, low, falling, high, rising,* respectively. When they have mastered this they then move onto the base tones for High and Low Class consonants. All other words are then compared against these base tones to ensure correctness.

Bear in mind that the tone for High Class and Low Class consonants are calcu-lated in a different manner to that of Middle Class consonants. This is covered in detail in section 5.

When learning the language, getting the tone correct can be one of the hardest tasks facing Westerners. However, don't be put off by speaking Thai. *Kon Tai* (Thai people) are very friendly and love to hear foreigners using their language and, if you ask them, would love to help you with pronunciation, new words, etc. At the very least you could cheer up someone's day - just persevere, it's well worth it.

Tone Graph

The following graph provides further explanation of tone pitch:

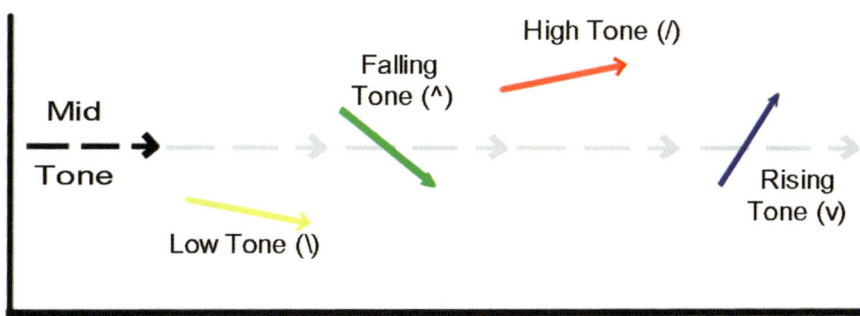

Here you can see the tone ranges in the order that Thai students learn them. The grey mid tone line gives you a reference for pitch levels.

2. Consonants

In the Thai alphabet there can be more than one consonant character for a particular sound. For example, there are six consonants that make the /k/ sound, five as an *initial consonant*[2] and one as a *final consonant.* Therefore, there has to be a method to be able to differentiate between consonants.

---

2. *Though two are now obsolete.*

To do this every Thai consonant has a name that gives us the sound the consonant makes and its distinguishing name. This name is comprised of three component parts:

1. The sound that the consonant makes; this is <u>always</u> the first or a combination of the first *and* second letters of the consonant name, e.g. /g/, /k/, /ng/, /ch/, etc.
2. An inherent vowel (this appears in every consonant); and
3. a noun that identifies the consonant.

The first consonant of the Thai alphabet is called Gɔɔ Gài. We mentioned the Paiboon Transliteration System in the introduction and the 'ɔɔ' characters in the first word are part of this. These characters describe the vowel sound that this word makes.

This particular sound is like the *aw* in the word *awe*. The standard convention for writing the sound is /-/. So, for Gɔɔ Gài, the Gɔɔ part is pronounced /g/ +/aw/ and it is written as /gɔɔ/.

Golden Triangle, N Thailand

You will see some other unfamiliar characters in the List of Consonants and Sounds, Table 2.1.1. These characters and the sounds they make are all explained in Table 3.1.1 (page 18) and Table 3.1.2 (on page 19) under the section on vowels.

Gɔɔ Gài is written as ก ไก่ and it is comprised of:

- ก – the consonant. This consonant makes the 'G' sound (g as in 'gate'. Using the above convention, we write this as /g/).
- The 'ɔɔ' part. This is an inherent part of every consonant and transforms the consonant sound into a word. It comes from the consonant ɔɔ Àang (อ อ่าง) (ɔɔ Àang is covered in more detail in section 8.2).
- ไก่ (Gài) – this is the name of the 'item' the consonant refers to.
  Gài means *chicken* and is comprised of:
  - the vowel ไ-, giving the vowel sound /ai/ (like the *ie* part of the word *lie*);
  - the consonant ก, giving the consonant sound /g/; and
  - the tone mark ่ (above the ก).
  Tone marks and tones are covered in section 5 but, for this particular word, this tone mark makes the word **low tone**.

When we wish to give an example without using a specific consonant, we mark the consonant position with a hyphen (-). In this example, the vowel สระ ไ- (sà-rà /ai/) is written before the consonant ก.

In written Thai, vowels can be above, below, before and after the consonant; this particular vowel is *always* written before the consonant. Irrespective of where the vowel is written, the consonant sound is always pronounced first, i.e. ไก is pronounced /g/ + /ai/ = /gai/ not /ai/ + /g/ = /aig/. This is covered in detail in section 7 (The tone mark above ก has been deliberately omitted here).

2.1 Consonant List

The following table is the complete list of Thai consonants, their order, transliterated text name, meaning, the sound that they make and the class of the consonant.

In Thai, every consonant belongs to one of three classes: these are called High, Middle or Low [class]. This consonant class is used to help us calculate the syllable tone (refer to Tones in section 5).

Table 2.1.1 - List of Consonants and Sounds

No.	Thai Character	Transliterated Text Name	Meaning	Sound	As In...	Class (H, M, L)
1	ก ไก่	Gɔɔ Gài	Chicken	/g/	goal	Middle
2	ข ไข่	Kɔ̌ɔ Kài	Egg	/k/	kick	High
3	ฃ ขวด	Kɔ̌ɔ Kùat	Bottle	/k/	kick	High
4	ค ควาย	Kɔɔ Kwaai	Water Buffalo	/k/	kick	Low
5	ฅ คน	Kɔɔ Kon	Person	/k/	kick	Low
6	ฆ ระฆัง	Kɔɔ Rá-kang	Bell	/k/	kick	Low
7	ง งู	Ngɔɔ Nguu	Snake	/ng/	ringing	Low
8	จ จาน	Jɔɔ Jaan	Plate	/j/	joker	Middle
9	ฉ ฉิ่ง	Chɔ̌ɔ Chìng	Cymbals	/ch/	chop	High
10	ช ช้าง	Chɔɔ Cháang	Elephant	/ch/	chop	Low
11	ซ โซ่	Sɔɔ Sôo	Chain	/s/	sea	Low
12	ฌ เฌอ	Chɔɔ Chəə	Tree	/ch/	chop	Low
13	ญ หญิง	Yɔɔ Yǐng	Woman	/y/	yacht	Low
14	ฎ ชฎา	Dɔɔ Chá-daa	Head-dress	/d/	dog	Middle
15	ฏ ปฏัก	Dtɔɔ Bpà-dtàk	Spear	/dt/	stop	Middle

Table 2.1.1 - List of Consonants and Sounds

16	ฐ ฐาน	Tɔ̌ɔ Tăan	Pedestal	/t/	trim	High
17	ฑ มณโฑ	Tɔɔ Montoo	Giant's Wife	/t/	trim	Low
18	ฒ ผู้เฒ่า	Tɔɔ Pûu-tâo	Old Man	/t/	trim	Low
19	ณ เณร	Nɔɔ Neen	Monk	/n/	night	Low
20	ด เด็ก	Dɔɔ Dèk	Child	/d/	deck	Middle
21	ต เต่า	Dtɔɔ Dtào	Turtle	/dt/	stop	Middle
22	ถ ถุง	Tɔ̌ɔ Tǔng	Bag	/t/	trim	High
23	ท ทหาร	Tɔɔ Tá-hǎan	Soldier	/t/	trim	Low
24	ธ ธง	Tɔɔ Tong	Flag	/t/	trim	Low
25	น หนู	Nɔɔ Nǔu	Mouse	/n/	night	Low
26	บ ใบไม้	Bɔɔ Bai-mái	Leaf	/b/	ball	Middle
27	ป ปลา	Bpɔɔ Bplaa	Fish	/bp/	spot	Middle
28	ผ ผึ้ง	Pɔ̌ɔ Pûng	Bee	/p/	pint	High
29	ฝ ฝา	Fɔ̌ɔ Fǎa	Lid	/f/	fall	High
30	พ พาน	Pɔɔ Paan	Tray	/p/	pint	Low
31	ฟ ฟัน	Fɔɔ Fan	Tooth	/f/	fall	Low
32	ภ สำเภา	Pɔɔ Sǎm-pao	Junk	/p/	pint	Low
33	ม ม้า	Mɔɔ Máa	Horse	/m/	mast	Low
34	ย ยักษ์	Yɔɔ Yák	Giant	/y/	yacht	Low
35	ร เรือ	Rɔɔ Rʉʉa	Boat	/r/	run	Low
36	ล ลิง	Lɔɔ Ling	Monkey	/l/	light	Low
37	ว แหวน	Wɔɔ Wɛ̌ɛn	Ring	/w/	watch	Low
38	ศ ศาลา	Sɔ̌ɔ Sǎa-laa	Tent	/s/	sea	High
39	ษ ฤษี	Sɔ̌ɔ Rʉʉ-sǐi	Hermit	/s/	sea	High
40	ส เสือ	Sɔ̌ɔ Sʉ̌ʉa	Tiger	/s/	sea	High
41	ห หีบ	Hɔ̌ɔ Hìip	Chest	/h/	hut	High
42	ฬ จุฬา	Lɔɔ Jù-laa	Star-shaped Kite	/l/	light	Low
43	อ อ่าง	ɔɔ Àang	Bowl	/ɔɔ/	awe	Middle
44	ฮ นกฮูก	Hɔɔ Nók-hûuk	Owl	/h/	hug	Low

As you can see from the table, some sounds are made by more than one consonant. To avoid confusion, when referring to a consonant, its full name is always used, e.g. Gɔɔ Gài, Kɔ̌ɔ Kài, etc.

For example, คนจน. There are two words here, คน+จน (Thai script has few spaces in it). These are pronounced *kon jon* and mean *poor man* : kon = *person*, jon = *poor*. If you had to spell these out, you would spell them, "*kɔɔ kwaai, nɔɔ nǔu, jɔɔ jaan, nɔɔ nǔu*".

Pranburi, Prachuap Khiri Khan Province

At this stage it is unlikely that you would have noticed that all the letters here are consonants yet when you pronounce, "*kon jon*", you hear two vowels: an /o/ in both *kon* and *jon*. In Thai, in addition to written vowels, there are unwritten vowels (these will be covered in section 7.2).

Note: It may help you to think of the Thai alphabet in the same way we learn the Roman alphabet, e.g. where we think of A, /ei[3]/ Alpha; B, /biː/, Bravo; C, /ciː/ Charlie, try and think "*G, /gɔɔ/ Gài; K, /kɔ̌ɔ/ Kài; K, /kɔ̌ɔ/ Kùat.*"

2.2 Final Consonant Sounds

The sounds shown in Table 2.1.1 are called *initial consonant* sounds. If there are *initial consonant* sounds then it makes sense that there are also *final consonant* sounds: there are, eight of them: /ng/ (ง), /n/ (น), /m/ (ม), /i/ (ย), /o/ (ว), /k/ (ก), /t/ (ด), /p/ (บ).

With 44 consonants making just 21 initial consonant sounds and only 8 final consonant sounds it means that some consonants must have different *initial* and *final* sounds.

For example, the word บุญ (bun, meaning *merit* or *virtue*) has Bɔɔ Bai-mái (บ) as the initial consonant (/b/), a vowel beneath the initial consonant (◌ุ) giving us the /u/ sound; and Yɔɔ Yǐng (ญ) as the final consonant. Though Yɔɔ Yǐng has an initial consonant sound of /y/, its sound when a final consonant is /n/.

---

[3] *Using the Cambridge phonetic system.*

It is necessary to know the final consonant sound for a syllable in order to determine the correct tone. These eight *final consonant sounds* are further divided into *sonorant* and *stop* finals.

2.2.1 Sonorant and Stop Finals

Sonorant Finals

Sonorant finals are sounds that are fully voiced, e.g. the words, *song* or *drum*. When you say these you will feel your larynx vibrate (get a native Thai speaker to help you if you need to). There are five sonorant finals in the Thai language.

Table 2.2.1 - Sonorant Finals

Consonant	Final Sound
ง	/ng/
ญ ณ น ร ล and ฬ	/n/
ม	/m/
ย	/i/
ว	/o/

As can be seen in the table above, the final consonant sound /n/ is made by six consonants.

The following list shows examples of words containing the sonorant final consonants listed above:

- วาง (waang - *put down, place*)
- พาน (paan - *tray*)
- หาร (hăan - *divide, share*)
- ผอม (pɔ̆ɔm - *thin, slim*)
- คอย (kɔɔi - *wait*)
- กาว (gaao - *glue, gum*).

Stop Finals

The three stop final consonant sounds are unaspirated. Think of saying the word *stop!* The /p/ is aspirated. If you unaspirate/shorten the 'p', so it sounds more like 'b' the word becomes similar to *stob;* the letter is still **p** but there is no final stress on the final consonant.

The following table shows the stop final consonants and their corresponding sounds.

Table 2.2.2 - Stop Finals

Consonant	Final Sound
ก ข ค and ฆ	/k/
จ ฉ ช ซ ฌ ฎ ฏ ฐ ฑ ฒ ด ต ถ ท ธ ศ ษ and ส	/t/
บ ป ผ ฝ พ ฟ and ภ	/p/

For example:

• มาก (mâak - *much, a lot*)
• นาค (nâak - *mythological serpent*)
• บาด (bàat - *cut*)
• ประเทศ (bprà-têet - *country, nation*)
• ชอบ (chɔ̂ɔp - *like*)
• ปรารภ (bpraa-róp - introduction, remark or express concern).

Note: even though all consonants have a final sound, not all consonants are used in the final position. Unfortunately, you still need to learn them.

(Refer to Appendix A for the full list of initial and final consonant sounds).

3. Vowels

Vowel is pronounced sà-rà (ส-ระ) in Thai and is followed by the vowel name/sound itself, e.g. sà-rà am (-ำ) is written สระ -ำ and the vowel sound is written as /am/ (though it sounds similar to /um/ as in *umbrella*).

There are two types of basic vowel: short vowel and long vowel. Vowel length is one of the factors that can be used to determine syllable tone (refer to section 5.4, Determining Tone).

Vowel sounds are written in the same way as consonant sounds but we need a method to differentiate between short and long. We do this with simple vowels by repeating the vowel sound when it is long, e.g. for sà-rà a (สระ -ะ), a short vowel, we write /a/; and for sà-rà aa (สระ -า), a long vowel, we write /aa/.

Note: The majority of the time, the sound is the same and it's just a longer vowel (approximately 2-3 times as long as a rough guide). But, as with any pronunciation, if you are unsure, it is advisable to seek assistance from a Thai friend.

3.1 Short and Long Vowels

Thai vowels can be placed in front of, above, after and below a consonant. If no consonant is present, the hyphen (-) is used to represent where a consonant would be written [in relation to the vowel]. The following table lists all the common, long and short simple vowels:

Table 3.1.1 - Short and Long Vowels

Short Vowel			Long Vowel		
Vowel	Sound	Sounds Like	Vowel	Sound	Sounds Like
The 4 vowels to the right can be short or long but are considered long for tone purposes.			-ํา	/am/	b**um**p
			ใ-	/ai/	l**ie**
			ไ-	/ai/	l**ie**
			เ-า	/ao/	m**ou**se
-ะ	/a/	m**u**ll	-า	/aa/	p**a**lm
ิ	/i/	p**i**t	ี	/ii/	sh**ee**p
ึ	/ɤ/	p**u**t	ื	/ɤɤ/	m**oo**n
ุ	/u/	p**u**t	ู	/uu/	m**oo**n
เ-ะ	/e/	b**e**t	เ-	/ee/	b**e**d
แ-ะ	/ɛ/	b**a**t	แ-	/ɛɛ/	b**a**d
โ-ะ	/o/	n**o**t	โ-	/oo/	g**oa**t
เ-าะ	/ɔ/	n**o**t	-อ	/ɔɔ/	**aw**e

Some vowel sounds have no comparable sound in English and all given examples are sounds as close to the Thai sounds as the English language allows.

Particularly different (and difficult) are sà-rà /ɤ/ and /ɤɤ/. The sound for these has to come from your throat, similar to when you burp. The sound must be kept short (/ɤ/, but longer with /ɤɤ/) and it must come from the throat (not the mouth). Also, your mouth should be open slightly (just!).

You may have noticed that in the table there are two vowels that make the /ai/ sound:

• Sà-rà ai mái-má-lai (ไ-), and
• Sà-rà ai mái-múan (ใ-).

Both produce the same sound but there are only twenty occurrences of sà-rà ai mái-múan (ไ-) in the Thai language. For a list of these words, refer to Appendix C.2.

Listed in Table 3.1.2 are the remaining 12 vowels. These vowels are formed by combining two or more short or long vowels. These are not as common as those shown in Table 3.1.1.

Table 3.1.2 - Complex Vowels

Short Vowel			Long Vowel		
Vowel	**Sound**	**Sounds Like**	**Vowel**	**Sound**	**Sounds Like**
เ-อะ	/ə/	**a**bove	เ-อ	/əə/	**ea**rly
เ-ียะ	/ia/	**r**ia	เ-ีย	/iia/	r**ea**l
เ-ือะ	/ɯa/	n**ewe**r	เ-ือ	/ɯɯa/	br**ewe**r
-ัวะ	/ùa/	b**ua**t	-ัว	/ua/	t**ou**r
ฤ	/rɯ/	**roo**k	ฤๅ	/rɯɯ/	**roo**t
ฦ	/lɯ/	**loo**k	ฦๅ	/lɯɯ/	**loo**t

3.2   Consonants and Vowels / Vowel Sounds

There are three consonants in the Thai alphabet that can function as consonants, vowels or provide vowel sounds: Yɔɔ Yák (ย), Wɔɔ Wɛ̌ɛn (ว) and ɔɔ Àang (อ).

They form the following vowel sounds:

Table 3.2.1 Consonant Vowel Sounds

Consonant	Initial Consonant Sound	Final Consonant or Vowel Sound
Wɔɔ Wɛ̌ɛn (ว)	/w/	/o/ or /oo-a/
ɔɔ Àang (อ)	/ɔɔ/	/ɔɔ/
Yɔɔ Yák (ย)	/y/	/i/

Wɔɔ Wɛ̌ɛn (ว) and ɔɔ Àang (อ) can be used as vowels in their own right, i.e. on their own.

However, Yɔɔ Yák (ย) provides a vowel <u>sound</u> when it is in the final consonant position but it is never a vowel when <u>on its own</u>: it has to combine with another vowel to form a complex vowel sound, e.g.

- กาว (gaao - *gum, glue*)
- ยาว (yaao - *long*)
- ห่อ (hɔ̀ɔ - *parcel, package*)
- พ่อ (pɔ̂ɔ - *father*)
- ยาย (yaai - *grandmother*)
- นาย (naai - *Mr.*)
- เนย (nəəi - *butter*).

Note: The actual sound that เ-ย makes is diffcult to express in English. The closest vowel sound is /əəi/ as in day.

In these few short pages you've been faced with 44 consonants, stop final consonants and sounds, sonorant finals, 32 vowels, monothongs, dipthongs, tripthongs, etc. Remember, as with all sections of this book, don't expect to learn it all at once, take your time, work on those parts you are comfortable with and use the other areas as guides or for background reading. Go at your own pace!

Erawan Waterfall, Kanchanaburi Province

Speaking Thai

4. Grammar (Wai-yaa-gɔɔn, ไว-ยา-กรณ์)

The sentence structure in Thai is the same as the sentence structure used in the English language:

Subject + Verb + Object

For example: *He likes rugby - kăo chɔ̂ɔp rák-bîi* (เขา ชอบ รัก-บี้)

However, there are a number of differences in other grammar areas, we'll cover the main ones here.

Articles

Thai does not use articles *a, an* or *the*, e.g. "*Where is the dog?*", is "*Where is dog*" or actually "*dog is where?*" (*sù-nák yùu tîi năi* - สุ-นัข อยู่ ที่ ไหน).

---
*
*There are no **hyphens** in Thai script, none. Everyone you see in this book has been added to aid you in identifying and reading Thai script.*

4.1 Verbs and Tense

There are no verb, noun or pronoun inflections in Thai and when you are talking about numbers, case, tense or gender change, etc., additional words are used to indicate the exact meaning.

For example, verb tense itself does not change but the meaning is determined by the addition of extra word(s). Using the expression, *I drink beer...* pŏm dùum biia (ผม ดื่ม เบียร์) as an example:

1. Present Tense

   If you are in the process of doing something the word *gamlang* (gam-lang (กำลัง)) is used, e.g.

   I am drinking beer - pŏm gam-lang dùum biia (ผม กำ-ลัง ดื่ม เบียร์)

2. Past Tense

   If you have finished an action, i.e. it is complete, you use the word *already* - lέεo (แล้ว) at the end of the sentence, e.g.

   I drank beer - pŏm dùum biia lέεo (ผม ดื่ม เบียร์ แล้ว).

3. Future Tense

   If an action is going to happen in the future then we precede the verb with *will* - jà (จะ).

   I will (or I shall) drink beer - pŏm jà dùum biia (ผม จะ ดื่ม เบียร์)

4.2 To Be

In English, we use the verb '*To be*' for a number of different situations such as "*I am 21 years old*," or, "*I am over here!*"

Thai has four methods of referring to '*to be*':

1. *yùu* (อยู่), is used when referring to a place or location.
2. *bpen* (เป็น), is used when referring to someone or something.
3. *kʉʉ* (คือ), is also used when referring to someone or something.
4. *mii* (มี), is used similar to "*There is/there are*".

4.2.1 Location

Yùu (อยู่) is used when we are referring to a place or a location, for example:

- "I am over here," - *pǒm yùu tîi nîi* (ผม อยู่ ที่ นี่)
- "Where are you?" - *kun yùu tîi nǎi* (คุณ อยู่ ที่ ไหน).

4.2.2 Someone or Something

Bpen (เป็น) and *kʉʉ* (คือ) are used when talking about someone or something. They should only be used when linking a pronoun or a noun to another noun.

First of all, neither *bpen* or *kʉʉ* are utilised as linking verbs when used with an adjective. For example, using the sentence, "*I am hungry.*"

If you said "*pǒm bpen hǐʉ*" (ผม เป็น หิว) (pronoun + verb + adjective), this would be incorrect, the correct saying is "*pǒm hǐʉ*" (ผม หิว), "I hungry."

You wouldn't use *kʉʉ* (คือ) for the same reason.

Kʉʉ

Kʉʉ is used when referring to a noun or when you need to describe the meaning of the noun; it is also used similar to *e.g.* or *i.e.* in English. For example:

- "*Nîi kʉʉ à-rai?,*" (นี่ คือ อะ-ไร) - "*What is this?*"
- "*Nîi kʉʉ bpàak-gaa,*" (นี่ คือ ปาก-กา) - "*This is a pen.*"
- "*Gâo-îi kʉʉ à-rai,*" (เก้า-อี้ คือ อะไร) - "*What is a chair?*"
- "*Gâo-îi kʉʉ tîi-nâng sǎm-ràp nʉng kon sǎa-mâat klʉ̂ʉan-yáai dâi,*" (เก้า-อี้ คือ ที่-นั่ง สำ-หรับ 1 คน สา-มารถ เคลื่อน-ย้าย ได้) - "*A chair is a moveable seat for one person to sit on.*"
- "*Nîi kʉʉ bâan kǒɔng chǎn,*" (นี่ คือ บ้าน ของ ฉัน) - "*This is my home.*"
- "*Nân kʉʉ rót kǒɔng krai,*" (นั่น คือ รถ ของ ใคร) - "*Whose car is that?*"

Bpen

Bpen is used when the subject and object are related. It is always used with occupation, nationality, disease, status/position or ownership, e.g.

- *"Kǎo bpen nák-bin,"* (เขา เป็น นัก-บิน) - *"He is a pilot."*
- *"Pǒm bpen nák-riian,"* (ผม เป็น นัก-เรียน) - *"I am a student."*
- *"Kǎo bpen kon jiin,"* (เขา เป็น คน จีน) - *"He is Chinese."*
- *"Chǎn bpen kâi,"* (ฉัน เป็น ไข้) - *"I have a fever."*
- *"Pǒm bpen kon sòot,"* (ผม เป็น คน โสด) - *"I am single."*
- *"Nân bpen rót kǒɔng krai,"* (นั่น เป็น รถ ของ ใคร) - *"Whose car is that?"*

You can see that the last example here is also used in the list under *kʉʉ*. There is a fine line between using *kʉʉ* and *bpen* and this comes with experience.

4.2.3 Mii

Mii (มี) is used in simple tense sentences where the meaning is *there is, there are, has, have,* etc. For example:

"Mii nák-riian yîi-sìp kon nai chán-riian." (มี นัก-เรียน ยี่-สิบ คน ใน ชั้น-เรียน) - *"There are twenty students in class."*

- *"Kǎo mii nák-riian yîi-sìp kon nai chán-riian."* (เขา มี นัก-เรียน ยี่-สิบ คน ใน ชั้น-เรียน) - *"She has twenty students in class."*

4.3 Questions

In Thai language, the only difference between an affirmative and an interrogative sentence is the interrogative sentence uses an interrogative word either at the beginning or, more commonly, at the end of a sentence.

For example, the affirmative sentence, *"You work hard,"* (*kun tam ngaan nàk -* คุณ ทำ งาน หนัก) becomes the interrogative sentence by adding the question word, *"Nǒ"* at the end of the sentence.

This then becomes, *"Do you work hard?"* or actually, *"You work hard, no?"* (*kun tam ngaan nàk mǎi -* คุณ ทำ งาน หนัก ไหม).

4.4 Possession

The words *bpen kɔ̌ɔng* (เป็น ของ) - *belong* are used to indicate ownership or possession of an object or item.

For example, mine is *kɔ̌ɔng pǒm/chǎn* (ของ ผม/ฉัน), yours is *kɔ̌ɔng kun* (ของ คุณ), his/hers is *kɔ̌ɔng kǎo* (ของ เขา), etc.

To say, "*The book is his*," or, "*The book belongs to him,*" would be *năng-sŭu bpen kɔ̌ong kǎo* (หนัง-สือ เป็น ของ เขา).

4.5 Adjectives

Adjectives come after the noun that they are modifying, e.g. *The red car* becomes '*car red*' - *rót sĭi-dɛɛng* (รถ สี-แดง).

When Thai people speak to each other they will very often leave out words if the meaning of their sentence is unambiguous.

This can be confusing to a learner but is common in many languages, e.g. "Where is the bathroom?" (*hɔ̂ong nám yùu tîi nǎi* - ห้อง น้ำ อยู่ ที่ ไหน), can be heard as just, "*Hɔ̂ong nám yùu nǎi.*"

Here we have the Thai words for bathroom, *hɔ̂ong nám: hɔ̂ong* (ห้อง) means room and *nám* (น้ำ) means water.

Similarly, the word for sleep is *nɔɔn* (นอน). Therefore the sleeping room, the bedroom, is *hɔ̂ong nɔɔn* (ห้อง นอน). The word for food is *aa-hǎan* (อา-หาร) and the dining or eating room is *hɔ̂ong aa-hǎan* (ห้อง อา-หาร).

5. Tone

Thai is a tonal language and, as was mentioned before, every <u>syllable</u> has one of 5 tones: Low, Mid, High, Rising and Falling.

You may think that it would be logical for tone class to coincide with consonant class, e.g. high tone = high class consonants, low tone = low class but, unfortunately, it doesn't!

Consonant class is an arbitrary classification that is used to group the consonants. It may well happen that a *syllable* with a middle class consonant is pronounced mid tone but this is due to other factors and not solely because of the consonant class.

Four factors affect the tone of a syllable:

1. If the syllable has a tone mark above the initial consonant (section 5.1).

2. The class of the consonant (section 5.2)

3. The vowel length (section 3.1)

4. Whether the end [consonant] sound is a *live syllable* or a *dead syllable* (section 5.3).

First of all, we'll look at tone marks.

5.1 Tone Marks

There are four tone marks in Thai script. A tone is called mái (ไม้) and then followed by the name of the tone. With the exception of consonant clusters (covered in Appendix C.4) tone marks are always written above the initial consonant of a syllable [or a superscript vowel if present].

The following table shows the tone marks used in Thai script.

Table 5.1.1 -Tone Marks

Tone Mark	Name		When written above the consonant class (shown below), that syllable will produce the tone shown:		
			Low Class	Middle Class	High Class
่	Mái èek	ไม้ เอก	Falling Tone (ˆ)	Low (ˋ)	Low (ˋ)
้	Mái too	ไม้ โท	High Tone (ˊ)	Falling (ˆ)	Falling (ˆ)
๊	Mái dtrii	ไม้ ตรี	High (ˊ)		
๋	Mái jàt-dtà-waa	ไม้ จัต-วา	Rising Tone (ˇ)		

Note: When a tone mark is present, *it overrules all other tone rules*.

For example: the word ป่า (pronounced bpàa, low tone) means '*forest, jungle*' and is comprised of *Bpɔɔ Bplaa* (ป), *mái èek* (่) and *sà-rà* aa (-า).

Bpɔɔ Bplaa (ป) is a Middle Class consonant and, from the table above, we see a Middle Class consonant + mái èek = **low tone**.

Scorpion Memorial to King Naruesan, Mae Sai, Northern Thailand

Once you have learnt the tone mark rules, it is fairly easy to see what the tone of a particular syllable will be.

The main problem is that if no tone mark is present then the tone has to be calculated. This is incredibly slow at first and can be a major hurdle.

In English, when we learn a word we have to remember the pronunciation, the spelling and the meaning; Thai is exactly the same but you must place additional emphasis on learning the correct tone.

Aids to Memory I - Tone Marks

Many find it difficult to remember the tone/tone mark rules so I've included the following images and 'stories' to assist you; these are the memory aids that I created and use, I hope they help.

Bear in mind that all memory aids are there to help you learn and recall information. If these don't make sense to you then no problem, just try and come up with your own.

- **Mái èek** (˗) -this looks like a bomb dropped from a warplane.

   When the plane flies on *high* or *middle* altitude bombing missions (*high* or *middle* class consonants) the bomb explodes at *low level* (read *low tone*).

   When the plane is on a *low* altitude bombing mission (read *low* class consonant) it uses pinpoint accuracy and can drop the bomb into holes and the bomb *falls* deeper into the ground (read *falling* tone).

   Therefore:

   Middle & High [class consonants] = **Low** [tone]; **Low** [class consonant]= **Falling** [tone].

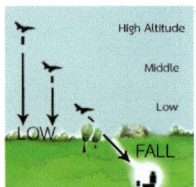

- **Mái too** (˘) - imagine this as the head of a sickle (or a scythe) used in the Russian revolution.

   The **low class** peasants revolt and the *middle* and *high* classes *fall* from grace; the *low* classes now elevate themselves to become *high* class.

   Therefore: **Middle & High = Falling, Low =** [the new] **High.**

- **Mái dtrii** (ʹ́) - imagine this shape as a crown on the head of royalty - the *high*est level in social status (**high** tone).

- **Mái jàt-dtà-waa** (ʹ̌)- this is like a *rising* star, twinkling in the night sky (**rise** [ing] tone).

5.2 Consonant Classes

Every consonant is categorised by being either Low, Middle or High class. Again, this is an arbitrary classification that is used alongside other factors, to

help determine the tone of a syllable (section 5.4).

In this book, to assist you we colour code all our consonants. It is a colour code that you will never forget as it is something that all of us see on a daily basis.

- Red is High [class]
- Yellow is Middle [class]
- Green is Low [class]

5.3 Live and Dead Syllables

We have spoken about sonorant final consonants, stop final consonants, short vowels and long vowels, now we need to understand live and dead syllables.

- A **dead syllable** is a syllable that ends with a **short vowel** or ends with a **stop final** consonant.
- A **live syllable** is a syllable that ends with a **long vowel** or a **sonorant final** consonant.

For example:

- จะ (jà – *will*). Sà-rà a (-ะ /a/) is a short vowel (Table 3.1.1), therefore this is a dead syllable.
- จัด (jàt – *arrange, prepare*). Dɔɔ Dèk (ด) is a stop final consonant (Table 2.2.2) and therefore this is a dead syllable.
- ไป (bpai – *go, leave*). Sà-rà ai (ไ- /ai/) is a long vowel (Table 3.1.1) and this is a live syllable.
- ยาว (yaao – *long*). Wɔɔ Wɛ̌ɛn (ว) is a sonorant final consonant (Table 2.2.1) and this is a live syllable.

5.4 Determining Tone

To reiterate, from section 5.1, where *tone marks are not present* we calculate tone from:

1. The class of the consonant (section 5.2 and Table 2.1.1)
2. Whether the vowel is short or long (section 3.1).
3. Whether the final consonant is a sonorant or stop final (section 2.2.1).

In addition, <u>for Low Class consonants only</u>, if the syllable is dead, the tone will depend on whether the vowel is short or long.

Table 5.4.1 - Calculating Tone

Syllable Type	Consonant Class		
	High Class	Middle Class	Low Class
Dead Syllables	Low Tone (\)	Low Tone (\)	Short Vowel: High Tone (/)
			Long Vowel: Falling Tone (^)
Live Syllables	Rising Tone (v)	Middle Tone	Middle Tone

For example:

- รับ (ráp – *receive*). Low Class consonant (Rɔɔ Rʉʉa - ร) + short vowel (-ั) + stop final consonant/dead syllable (Bɔɔ Bai-mái - บ) = High tone.
- มาก (mâak - *much, many*). Low Class consonant (Mɔɔ Máa - ม) + long vowel (-า) + stop final consonant/dead syllable (Gɔɔ Gài - ก) = Falling tone.
- ฟาง (faang – *straw*). Low Class consonant (Fɔɔ Fan - ฟ) + long vowel (–า) + sonorant consonant/live syllable (Ngɔɔ Nguu - ง) = Middle tone.

- ปิด (bpìt – *close, hide, shut, turn off*). Middle Class consonant (Bpɔɔ Bplaa - ป) + short vowel (◌ิ) + stop final consonant/dead syllable (Dɔɔ Dèk - ด) = Low tone.
- ขวา (kwǎa - *right*). High Class consonant (Kɔ̌ɔ Kài - ข) + long vowel/live syllable (◌า) = Rising tone.

At first, and understandably, the thought of remembering these tone rules may be a little daunting. There are some memory aids that I have created to help you.

Aids To Memory II - Tone Rules

Here are the acronyms that I use to remember the tone rules:

- Harry Drinks Lager (High [class consonant] + Dead [syllable] = Low [tone]) HDL
- Harry Likes Red Stripe (High + Live = Rising) HLR
- Mike Drinks Lager (Middle + Dead = Low) MDL
- Mike Likes Miller (Middle + Live = Middle) MLM
- Lesley Drinks SHandy (Low + Dead + Short [vowel] = High) LDSH
- Lesley Drinks Lager Fast (Low + Dead + Long [vowel] = Falling) LDLF
- Lesley Likes Miller (Low + Live = Middle) LLM.

Using the examples from section 5.4:

- รับ (ráp) - Low Class consonant + Dead syllable and Short vowel = High
- มาก (mâak) - Low Class consonant + Dead syllable and Long vowel = Falling
- ฟาง (faang) - Low Class consonant + Live syllable = Middle tone
- ปิด (bpìt) - Middle Class consonant + Dead syllable = Low
- ขวา (kwǎa) - High Class consonant + Live syllable = Rising.

Try and come up with your own.[4]

Note: These and all the memory aids for learning the consonants, verbs and tone rules can be found in the book by the same author: '*Memory Aids to Your Great Adventure*' at http://www.ltyga.com.

---

4. *The author supports the responsible consumption of alcohol.*

Please remember, this is an aid to memory whereas alcohol isn't. As you can see, we've used an orange font colour to represent middle class as yellow doesn't display particularly well on white paper.

Reading Thai

When most westerners look at Thai script for the first time they look for clues and for any resemblance between Thai character shapes and their 'own' alphabets.

The shapes are unfamiliar and there are additional strange characters written above the consonants. There are other 'weird' shapes written above those and few spaces between the words: very few clues and no familiar references.

Don't worry, all is not lost. In the following sections are some of the basic rules to help you.

6. Rules for Reading

One of the most confusing and off-putting features of Thai script is there are no spaces between words. Obviously the ability to identify syllables and words is fundamental to learning Thai.

There are a number of rules for reading Thai but an understanding of the following will enable you to make a good start in recognising where syllables and words start and end.

Learn these rules because you will be using these constantly. As you progress the process will become automatic but it does take a bit of time.

1. Every syllable starts with a consonant.

    Though the first character written in a syllable is not necessarily a consonant the consonant is <u>always</u> pronounced first.

2. A written vowel is always associated with a consonant.

    There are no 'free-standing' vowels, such as the vowels 'I' and 'A' in the English language. A vowel is always written 'around' a consonant.

3. A vowel is always written in the same place in relation to a consonant, it's position doesn't change.

    Some vowels are written before the consonant, some below, some above and some after: but they are always written in the same position (section 7.1).

4. Sà-rà ใ-, ไ-, -ะ and -า are never followed by a final consonant.

5. Sà-rà am (-ำ) always marks the end of a syllable.

6. The following vowel is always followed by a final consonant: -ี

That's it, six of them, now you can start reading Thai.

7. Vowels

When a vowel is written it must have a consonant associated with it. Irrespective of where the vowel is written, the consonant/consonant sound is always spoken first (rules 1 & 3 from the six you have just learnt): remember Gài (ไก่, from Gɔɔ Gài - section 2)?

The vowel sound is always the same, irrespective of the consonant it is used with, e.g. sà-rà /aa/ is always pronounced /aa/: gaa (กา - *crow*), raa (รา - *fungus*), maa (มา - *come*), etc.

First of all, we'll look at where vowels are written, this will help you in deciphering Thai script. In the following examples, once again, the hyphen (-) indicates the position where the consonant would be.

7.1 Where to Write Vowels

Vowels can be written before, above, below and after consonants.

Vowels Before

The following vowels always start a syllable:

เ -, แ -, โ -, ไ -, ใ-

e.g. เปิด (bpèət - *open, turn on*), แต่ (dtɛ̀ɛ - *but, since*), โมง (moong - *hour (daytime), o'clock*), ไม่ (mâi - *no*), ใจ (jai - *heart, mind, spirit*).

Vowels Above

These vowels are always written above a consonant:

◌ิ, ◌ี, ◌ึ, ◌ื, ◌ั

e.g. อิ่ม (ìm - *full up*), อีก (ìik - *again, more*), อึ้ง (ûng - *quiet, tongue-tied*), อืด (ùut - *slow, tardy*), ทั้ง (táng - *all, entire, whole*).

Vowels Below

These vowels are always written below a consonant:

◌ุ, ◌ู

e.g. ดุ (dù - *fierce, ferocious*), รู้ (rúu - *know (something)*).

Vowels After

The following vowels are always written after a consonant:

- ◌ะ, -า, ◌ำ

e.g. จะ (jà - *will*), หา (hǎa - *search*), จำ (jam - *remember, recall, recognise*).

32

Complex vowels are those that are comprised of more than one vowel. However, each component vowel part is still written in the same place. You just need to work out what the vowel/vowel sound is.

For example, the word *riian* (เรียน - *study*) uses the tripthong vowel sà-rà /iia/ (เ–ีย). Sà-rà เ-, sà-rà –ี and ย (Yɔɔ Yák) are written in their 'usual' place, you just need to remember the vowel sound.

If we replaced the ร in เรียน with ล (to give us เลียน, *liian* - *imitate, copy*) the vowel sound is exactly the same.

If you asked a Thai person to spell เรียน, you probably wouldn't hear "*Sà-rà /ee/, rɔɔ rʉʉa, sà-rà /ii/, yɔɔ yák, nɔɔ nǔu*", they would say "*Rɔɔ rʉʉa, sà-rà /iia/, nɔɔ nǔu.*" Clear, concise and little chance of error.

7.2 Unwritten Vowels

There are two unwritten vowels in Thai: sà-rà /o/ (โ-ะ), as in '*tot*' and sà-rà /a/ (-ะ), as in '*up*'

7.2.1 Same Syllable

Unwritten /o/ (โ-ะ) occurs between two consonants in the **same** syllable:

For example, in the personal pronoun ผม (pǒm - meaning '*I*', *me, used only by men*) and in ฝน (fǒn - meaning *rain*).

Note: when the final consonant is Rɔɔ Rʉʉa (ร) then the unwritten vowel between two same syllable consonants is changed from sà-rà /o/ to sà-rà /ɔɔ/.

Bath time!

For example:

- พร (*blessing*) is not pronounced /p/+/o/+/n/ it is pronounced /p/+/ɔɔ/+/n/ - /pɔɔn/.
- ศร (*arrow*) is pronounced /s/+/ɔ̌ɔ/ +/n/ - /sɔ̌ɔn/.

7.2.2 Different Syllable

Unwritten /a/ (-ะ) occurs between two **different** syllable consonants, e.g. สวัสดี (ส-วัส-ดี sà-wàt-dii - meaning *hello, good morning, good evening*, etc).

Note: With this different syllable rule, when the initial consonant of a syllable is Bɔɔ Bai-mái (บ) the unwritten vowel is pronounced /ɔɔ/ **not** /a/, e.g. wan pá-rʉ́-hàt-sà-**bɔɔ**-dii (วัน พ-ฤ-หั-ส-**บ**-ดี) - *Thursday*.

7.3 Mái Hǎn-aa-gàat

In the example above, we see the character ˘. This is called *mái hǎn-aa-gàat* (ไม้ หัน-อา-กาศ) and it gives us a [short] /a/ sound, which is the same as unwritten vowel sà-rà /a/ (-ะ).

Sà-rà /ua/ (-ัว)

Referring to Table 3.1.2, you will see that sà-rà /ua/ is comprised of *mái hǎn-aa-gàat* and *wɔɔ wɛ̌ɛn* (-ว).

When sà-rà /ua/ has a final consonant, *mái hǎn-aa-gàat* becomes an unwritten vowel; sà-rà /ua/ is still pronounced the same, e.g.

- รวย (ruai - *rich*)
- สวน (sǔan - *garden*)
- บวช (buat - *to ordain, become a monk*).

8. Silent Consonants

When you listen to Thai language you will hear vowel sounds being spoken without an apparent consonant sound. Now this may appear to contravene rules 1 & 2 (in section 6) but it doesn't: there are 'silent' consonants in the Thai alphabet.

Wat Arun, Bangkok

Although all syllables must start with a consonant (as per rule 1), some conso-nants can be silent (we write a silent consonant as /-/). As there is now a consonant present, a vowel can be placed (rule 2).

There are two consonants that can be silent: ɔɔ Àang (อ อ่าง) and Hɔ̌ɔ Hìip (ห หีบ). We will consider Hɔ̌ɔ Hìip first.

8.1 Hɔ̌ɔ Hìip

Hɔ̌ɔ Hìip (ห หีบ) is a High Class consonant that has two purposes. First of all, it produces the /h/ sound when spoken; secondly it is used to modify the class of consonants. In this latter capacity it becomes a 'silent' consonant (/-/).

Looking in detail at sections 5.1, Tone Marks and 5.4, Calculating Tone you will see it is not possible to have a low tone with a Low Class consonant.

The following table shows some Low Class consonants with their corresponding High Class [sounding] equivalents:

Low Class Consonant & Sound	Corresponding High Class Consonant & Sound
(ค) Kɔɔ Kwaai /k/	(ข) Kɔ̌ɔ Kài /k/
(ช) Chɔɔ Cháang /ch/	(ฉ) Chɔ̌ɔ Chìng /ch/

The following Low Class consonants do not have a High Class equivalent: ง, ญ, น, ม, ย, ร, ล, ว.

But, by using Hɔ̌ɔ Hìip, the Low Class *initial consonant* is replaced with a 'silent' High Class initial consonant and becomes a High Class syllable.

Example 1

ลาย (laai - *design, pattern*): Low Class [consonant] + Live [syllable] = Mid tone (LLM).

Whereas, by placing Hɔ̌ɔ Hìip in front of it, it now becomes:

หลาย (lǎai - *many, several*): High Class [consonant] + Live [syllable] = Rising tone (HLR).

Example 2

มาด (mâat – *appearance or manner*): Low Class + Dead syllable and Long vowel = Falling tone (LDLF).

Using Hɔ̌ɔ Hìip, it now becomes:

หมาด (màat - *almost dry*): High Class + Dead syllable = Low tone (HDL).

8.2 ɔɔ Àang

ɔɔ Àang (อ อ่าง) has a dual purpose: firstly it produces the /ɔɔ/ sound when spoken and secondly, it is used as a silent consonant/vowel (/-/).

We say consonant/vowel because although ɔɔ Àang is the 43rd consonant it actually acts more like a vowel than a consonant. The 'silent' characteristic enables it to be used as a *vowel placement consonant.*

We will show two examples of ɔɔ Àang:

1. acting as a voiced consonant/vowel
2. as a silent [vowel placement] consonant

8.2.1 ออ Àang as a Voiced Consonant/Vowel

- กอด (gòot). This word means *embrace* or *hug*.

    This is comprised of: Goo Gài (ก), ออ Àang (อ) and Doo Dèk (ด).

    Goo Gài as an initial consonant gives the /g/ sound; ออ Àang is voiced as /oo/; and Doo Dèk as a [stop] final consonant gives a /t/ sound.

    Tone rules state Middle Class consonant (ก) + Dead syllable (ด) = Low Tone (section 5.3 and section 5.4) (MDL).

    This word is pronounced /gòot/, low tone.

    Note: For this example, we have to ask ourselves what actually is ออ Àang doing here, is it a consonant or a vowel?

    If you remember, ออ Àang produces the /oo/ sound whether it is acting as a consonant or as a vowel (Table 2.1.1 or Table 3.1.1).

    Every Thai word needs at least one consonant and one vowel. If the อ in กอด is acting as a consonant then the word is comprised of three written consonants **and**, if you remember the unwritten vowel rules from section 7.2, it would also have to have two of these.

    This would then give us an unwritten /a/ between ก & อ and an unwritten /o/ between อ & ด. If we write this out phonetically it would be more like /g/ + /a/ + /oo/ + /o/ + /t/ (ga-oo-ot). This is clearly wrong. Therefore อ has to be acting as a vowel in this example.

8.2.2 ออ Àang as a Silent [Vowel Placement] Consonant

- อีก (ìik). The word means *again*.

    The /ii/ part of the word comes from [silent] ออ Àang (/-/) and the vowel sà-rà /ii/ (ี). The /k/ comes from Goo Gài (ก) acting as a final consonant.

    The word is pronounced Low tone: Middle Class consonant (อ) + Dead syllable (ก) = (MDL)

- อาหาร (อา-หาร - aa-hăan). This means *"food."*

    This word has two syllables. In the first syllable (อา), ออ Àang is silent and enables the placement of sà-rà aa (-า, /aa/).

    When the silent consonant is used, the only sound is the vowel sound /aa/.

    This syllable's tone is calculated as:

    Middle Class consonant (อ) + Live syllable (-า) = Mid tone (MLM)

The second syllable is หาร (/hǎan/).

The pronunciation of this syllable is straightforward and is pronounced rising tone:

High Class consonant (ห) + Live Syllable (remember Rɔɔ Rʉʉa as a final consonant gives the /n/ sonorant sound) = (HLR).

• อาหารเช้า (อา-หาร เช้า - aa-hǎan cháo). This three syllable word means *"breakfast"* and is derived from the Thai word for *food* and the word for *morning* (เช้า - cháo).

The last syllable is high tone from Low Class consonant (ช) + Mái Too (-́).

Note: the word for *noon/midday* is *tîiang* (เที่ยง), therefore *lunch* is *aa-hǎan tîiang*.

The Thai word for *dinner* is *aa-hǎan yen* (อาหาร เย็น) and this just needs a short explanation.

The word for evening is *dtɔɔn yen* (ตอน เย็น): *dtɔɔn* is a word commonly used to denote a time period, and *yen* means late afternoon, evening or dusk. *Dtɔɔn* is dropped when there is no ambiguity.

"Have you eaten yet?"

Rice is a huge part of Thai food culture and is eaten with most meals. You may hear some Thai people say, "*Gin kâao lɛ́ɛo rʉ̌ʉ yang?*" (กิน ข้าว แล้ว หรือ ยัง) when they meet a friend - as opposed to *sà-wàt-dii* (สวัสดี). This translates as "*Eat rice already yet,*" or "*Have you eaten yet?*" and was the traditional greeting before *sà-wàt-dii* was introduced. It is still used by some, mainly older, people today.

Breakfast can also be referred to as *kâao cháo* (ข้าว เช้า); lunch as *kâao tîiang* (ข้าว เที่ยง) and dinner as *kâao yen* (ข้าว เย็น).

ออ Àang Changing Consonant Class

Additionally, ออ Àang is seen as the first consonant in certain words such as:

• yàak (อยาก) - *would like*
• yàang (อย่าง) - *as, like*.

In both examples ออ Àang is acting as a silent consonant, similar to Hɔ̌ɔ Hìip, but each word now becomes Middle Class: without ออ Àang, each word would be Low Class (from the initial consonant Yɔɔ Yák).

Without ออ Àang we would have yâak (ยาก) - *hard, difficult* and yâang (ย่าง) - *grill*. Note the tones: falling tone for the former (remember LDLF), and falling tone for the latter (mái èek + low class consonant).

9. Shortening Vowels

Thai has two methods of shortening a word and its pronunciation: firstly, with ๊- (ไม้-ไต่-คู้) and, secondly, with - ะ (sà-rà /a/).

9.1 Mái-dtài-kúu (๊-)

The character ๊- is called mái-dtài-kúu (ไม้-ไต่-คู้).

Mái-dtài-kúu is used with the vowels sà-rà เ- (/ee/) and sà-rà แ- (/ɛɛ/) to shorten the word.

Shortening sà-rà เ-

Using the word เบน (been - *turn away, change direction*). Adding mái-dtài-kúu gives us เบ็น (Ben - *man's name*)

With one exception, mái-dtài-kúu must have a final consonant associated with it as the syllable cannot end with just ๊-; this exception is with the word ก็ (Gô – *also*). ก็ is pronounced with the inherent (อ) vowel sound.

As an aid to assist you in pronunciation, the length of the vowel when mái-dtài-kúu is used is similar to the length of saying the word '*n*' in English.

Shortening sà-rà แ-

แล็ปท็อป - this is how the word *laptop* is spelt in Thai (แล็ป-ท็อป - *lép-tóp*).

Wat Phra Sing Waramahawihan, Chiang Mai

9.2 Sà-rà a (-ะ)

The second method is by using -ะ (sà-rà /a/).

Sà-rà -ะ can be used to shorten the long แ- and other complex vowels (refer to Table 3.1.2), e.g. และ (lɛ́ - *and*): without the 'shortener' this word would be แล (lɛɛ - *look, see, glance*).

Sà-rà -ะ is <u>always</u> at the end of a syllable.

10. Last Consonant/First Consonant

As we have seen, there are a few consonants that have one sound as an initial consonant and a different sound as a final consonant. There are also a number of words in the language where words have been joined together and the final consonant of one syllable also acts as the initial consonant of the next. This way the consonant is written only once yet fulfils both the initial and final consonant position.

One example of this is in the word ผลไม้ (pŏn-lá-mái - *fruit*).

It is spelt as if it should be pŏn-mái (ผลไม้) but Lɔɔ Ling (ล) provides the final consonant sound /n/ at the end of the first syllable and then provides its initial consonant sound of /l/ for the middle syllable. The unwritten vowel /a/ (section 7.2) gives us the vowel for the middle syllable (ผน-ละ-ไม้ - this is how phonetic Thai is written - pŏn-lá-mái).

Another example is the word พจนานุกรม (pót-jà-naa-nú-grom - *dictionary*). Here, Jɔɔ Jaan provides the final consonant sound /t/ at the end of the first syllable and then its initial consonant sound /j/ for the second syllable (in phonetic Thai it is written as พด-จะ-นา-นุ-กรม).

You need to be aware that there are a number of words in Thai which do not conform to the rules shown. Without knowing the actual word itself, it is unlikely that you would be able to work out the correct pronunciation. In these cases you need to know the word and its meaning.

The Grand Palace, Bangkok

Writing Thai

If you have never written Thai script before then initially it will seem very difficult and cumbersome: this is, of course, purely due to a lack of familiarity and practice. My own experience was that I struggled with most of the characters, I was very slow, my handwriting looked untidy and scratchy and the end result was very unimpressive.

I persevered for a time but though I tried, I couldn't master the 'beak' of Gɔɔ Gài ; the 'loops' on Kɔɔ Rá-kang and Chɔɔ Chəə just tied me in knots; and, as for dɔɔ and dtɔɔ... well forget it!

Finally, I took a break, went outside and walked down the soi.

As the wafts of Pàd Tai, Gɛɛng Kǐiao Wǎan Gài, Sôm-dtam or Gǔai dtǐiao hit me from the many street vendors I glanced about and saw the many hand-written signs. It was then I realised that very few of us actually can or do write in the style of the Times New Roman or Bookman Old Style fonts [Thai-equivalent of course].

I then asked one of my Thai friends to help me. She showed me how to write the Thai characters and, with a little practice, it all came together.

11. How To Write Thai Characters

It is recommended that you start practising writing the Thai alphabet as soon as possible. In addition to familiarising yourself with the characters and the alphabet, it will also help you in creating your own learning lists or flashcards.

11.1 Consonant Practice

On the right hand page of each page spread, you will see a character drawn in the box:

Take a piece of tracing paper, cover the letter and then start drawing the shape of the character. For Gɔɔ Gài draw up, then down, up, down and keep going until you get the feel for the drawn shape (as shown on the next page). Then, put aside this book and, on a separate piece of paper, practise, practise, practise!

As you progress you will see that your lines become less wavy and tighter. In a short while you will find that you can draw the shape smaller, neater and faster: repetition is key.

Where consonants have loops, always try and start with the loop and, where possible, complete the consonant in one stroke.

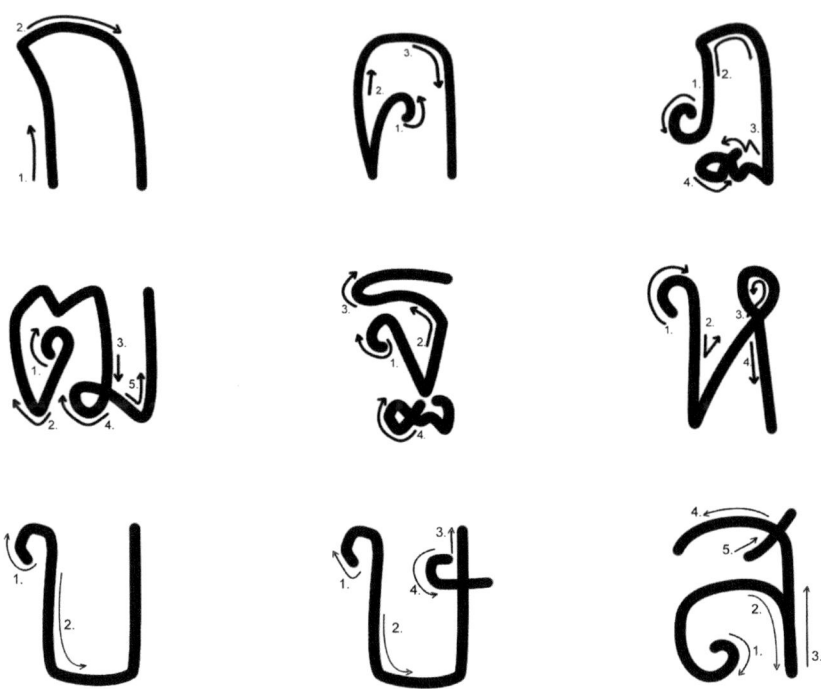

Note: When you draw a consonant, be aware of where the loop actually is. It will be to the left, the right, above or below the actual line you are drawing. Its position is very important as it is, in a number of cases, the only difference between writing Kɔɔ Kwaai (ค) and Dɔɔ Dèk (ด), or Kɔɔ Kon (ค) and Dtɔɔ Dtào (ต).

Try and master writing the consonants as they are written at the top of each page, it does take longer to learn but looks far neater.

11.2 Vowels

We won't cover writing vowels here as you'll be keen to start working through the story, refer to Appendix D for instructions on how to write the vowels correctly.

Page Layout

Now we will look at the layout of the story section. First of all the consonant main page.

12. Main Page

Each page spread of the book is one consonant of the Thai alphabet (as shown below).

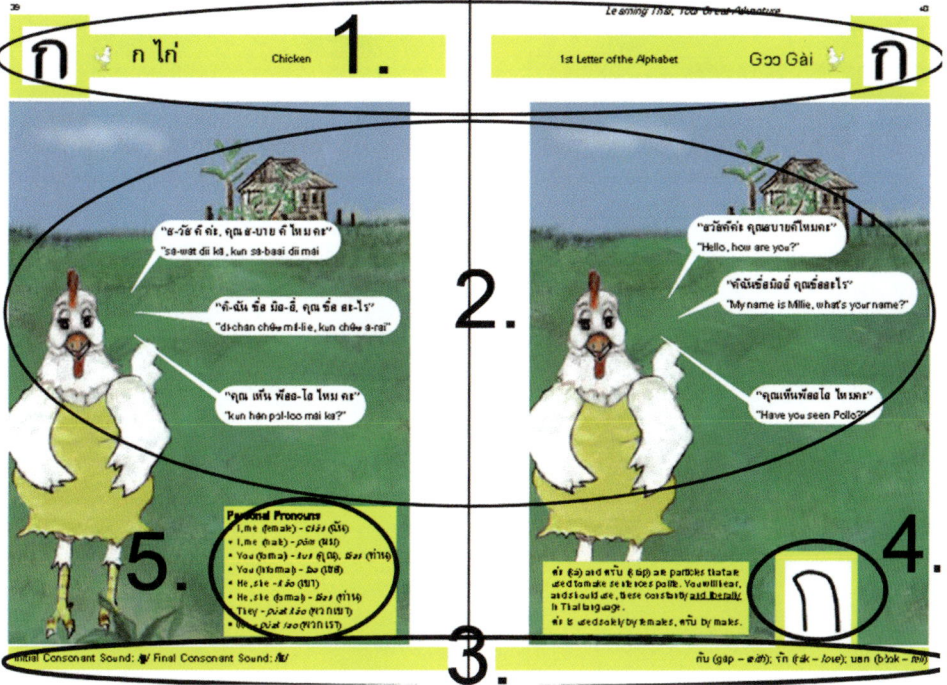

As you can see, it is broken down into five areas:

1. Header
2. Main dialogue
3. Footer
4. Writing Thai characters
5. Information Boxes.

The page is designed to ensure that all the information that you need is in front of you. It keeps you on the same page so that your concentration doesn't waver and your time is actually spent learning and not trying to find information.

12.1 Header

Your initial view shows you that the Header Bar is yellow. The colour of the bar is a memory aid to learning the consonant class. The yellow bar indicates this is a Middle Class consonant (section 5.2).

From the left you see:

1. The consonant character
2. A picture of the item, telling you what this item actually is, e.g. for Gɔɔ Gài, you see a picture of a chicken.
3. The name of the consonant (in Thai script): this is how you refer to it and how the word is pronounced.
4. The English meaning of the consonant letter.

Then, on the right hand page, still continuing on from the left:

5. Its position in the Thai alphabet (1 – 44, in English)
6. The transliterated name of the consonant
7. The picture
8. The consonant character.

12.2 Main Dialogue

Here we have the main dialogue of the book and there are two identical images facing you. First of all, we'll look at the left page.

12.2.1 Left Page

On the left page you have the information and dialogue given to you in transliterated Thai and in hyphenated, word spaced Thai script. This introduces a number of common phrases and frequently used words to you and enables easy viewing of each syllable and word in Thai and quick following of the dialogue.

The transliterated Thai helps you to understand how to say the word by showing you its breakdown by syllable and its pronunciation.

The Thai script has been hyphenated to help you view and learn the individual syllables and words. We have also inserted commas into the Thai script to match the comma break in the transliterated text. This helps you to match the transliterated pronunciation to the actual Thai word.

All of these are only to assist you at this early stage, *there are no hyphenations or punctuation* in actual Thai script.

Hyphenated words will never be 100% accurate because many Thai words have unwritten vowels (section 7.2). Placing a hyphen immediately after a consonant may lead you to believe that the consonant is providing its own inherent sound <u>and</u> the vowel sound, it isn't, it's the only way we can indicate it.

For example, with the word สวัสดี (sàwàtdii - *hello*). We break this down by syllable to 'sà-wàt-dii'.

We hyphenate the first syllable between ส and ว, to give ส-ว[สˋ-ดี]. However, the first syllable is pronounced /sà/ as there is an unwritten '*a*' between the two consonants that are in different syllables.

You cannot tag the unwritten 'a' in front of ว (as this would change the sound and the meaning of the word) so it has to read as if it belongs to the preceeding consonant, ส. However, writing it in this manner incorrectly gives the impression that Sɔ̌ɔ Sɛ̌ɯa <u>alone</u> is giving us the /sà/ sound, whereas in fact it comes from ส **and** ว. Alas there is no other effective method of hyphenation and you need to be aware of this when reading any hyphenated and transliterated Thai.

12.2.2 Right Page

The drawing on the right page is identical to that on the left but this time the dialogue is in Thai script, *exactly as it would be written*, with the English translation beneath it.

This layout enables you to concentrate on the left page at first, learning the Thai script, the word shapes and the pronunciation. Then, with just a quick glance you can see how it would actually be written and obtain the meaning of the words, phrase or sentence without leaving your double-page spread.

Once you become more proficient you can just ignore the left page and read the Thai script on the right.

12.3 Footer Bar

Shown in the Footer Bar on the left-page is the sound that the consonant makes. Some consonants have only one sound irrespective of whether they are an initial or final consonant, others have different sounds, one as an initial consonant and the other when they are in the final consonant position. These will be shown here.

On the right-hand page are common words that use this particular consonant. They are written in Thai script, transliterated Thai and English to help you to expand your vocabulary, to familiarise yourself with Thai script, and to practice.

12.4 Information Boxes

As you progress through the book you will see information boxes on some of the pages.

These boxes are there to provide additional information to assist you in learning the language, expanding your vocabulary and by providing various cultural and other useful information.

Let's continue with the consonant story .

Consonant Story

ก

 ก ไก่　　　　　　Chicken

"ส-วัส-ดี ค่ะ, คุณ ส-บาย ดี ไหม คะ"
"sà-wàt-dii kâ, kun sà-baai dii măi ká."

"ดิ-ฉัน ชื่อ มิล-ลี่, คุณ ชื่อ อะ-ไร"
"dì-chăn chน้ʉ míl-lie, kun chน้ʉ à-rai"

"คุณ เห็น พอล-โล่ ไหม คะ"
"kun hěn pɔɔl-lôo măi ká?"

Personal Pronouns
- I, me (female) - *chăn* (ฉัน)
- I, me (male) - *pŏm* (ผม)
- You (formal) - *kun* (คุณ), *tâan* (ท่าน)
- You (informal) - *təə* (เธอ)
- He, she - *kăo* (เขา)
- He, she (formal) - *tâan* (ท่าน)
- They - *púak kăo* (พวกเขา)
- We - *púak rao* (พวกเรา)

Initial Consonant Sound: /g/ Final Consonant Sound: /k/

Gɔɔ Gài

"สวัสดีค่ะ คุณสบายดีไหมคะ"

"Hello, how are you?"

"ดิฉันชื่อมิลลี่ คุณชื่ออะไร"

"My name is Millie, what's your name?"

"คุณเห็นพอลโล่ ไหมคะ"

"Have you seen Pollo?"

ค่ะ (kâ) and ครับ (kráp) are particles that are used to make sentences polite. You will hear and should use them constantly <u>and liberally</u> in Thai language. ค่ะ is used solely by females, ครับ by males.

ก

กับ (gàp – *with*); รัก (rák – *love*); บอก (bɔ̀ɔk – *tell*)

ข

ข ไข่   Egg

Thai uses **Subject + Verb + Object** for composing sentences.

Determiners, however, are rarely used, e.g. in English, we say, "A bottle and a letter!".

However in Thai it's, "kùat lέ jòt-mǎai" (ขวด และ จด-หมาย) - literally, *Bottle and letter*.

Consonant Sound: /k/

2nd Letter of the Alphabet　　　Kǎo Kài 　　ข

"สวัสดีค่ะ พอลโล่ คุณสบายดีไหมคะ"
"Hello Pollo, how are you?"

"ผมสบายดีครับ คุณสบายดีไหมครับ"
"I am well, how are you?"

"สบายดีค่ะ นั่นคุณได้อะไรคะ"
"Good, what do you have there?"

"ขวดและจดหมาย"
"A bottle and a letter!"

บ

โข (kǒo – *very*); เขา (kǎo – *he, she*); แข่ง (kɛ̀ɛng – *race*)

ซ ฃ ขวด Bottle

This Consonant is Obsolete.

3rd Letter of the Alphabet   Kɔ̌ɔ Kùat

ผมชื่อทอมมี่
My name is Tommy
ผมเป็นคนอังกฤษ
I am English.
ผมอายุ 20 ปี
I am 20 years old
ผมอยู่ที่ลอนดอน
I live in London.
ผมกำลังเรียนภาษาไทย
I am learning Thai language
นี่คืออีเมลของผม
Here is my email address:
Tommy_atkins@defdomain.net
ด้วยความนับถือ
Regards
ทอมมี่
Tommy

"จดหมายอะไรครับ"
"What does it say?"

"ฉันไม่รู้ค่ะ ถามแพนเค้กกันเถอะ"
"I don't know, let's ask Pancake"

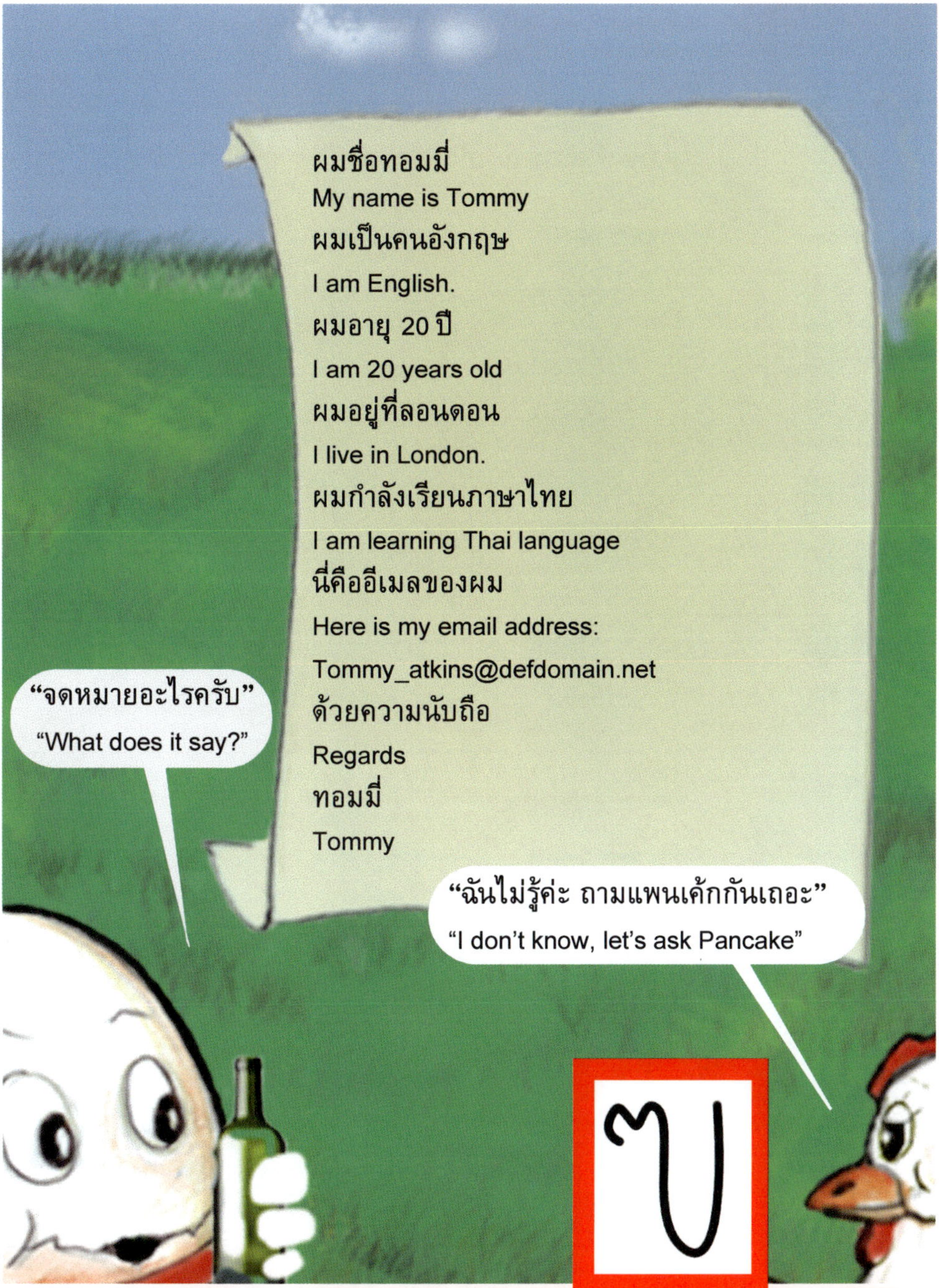

 **ค ควาย** Water Buffalo

"ส-วัส-ดี ค่ะ แพน-เค้ก, คุณ อ่าน จด-หมาย นี้ ได้ ไหม"
"sà-wàt-dii kâ pɛɛn-kéɛk, kun àan jòt-mǎai níi dâi mǎi?"

"เสีย-ใจ ครับ, ผม อ่าน ไม่ ได้"
"sǐia-jai kráp, pǒm àan mâi dâi."

"ผู้-หญิง ที่ บ้าน นั้น อาจ-จะ อ่าน ได้"
"pûu-yǐng tîi bâan nán àat-jà àan dâi."

"เป็น ความ คิด ที่ ดี ขอบ-คุณ ค่ะ"
"bpen kwaam kít tîi dii kɔ̀ɔp-kun kâ."

Question?

Instead of question marks (?), Thai uses a number of *question particles*, including ไหม (mǎi); mǎi loosely means 'No?'

In the dialogue above, Millie's question uses the particle dâi mǎi (ได้ ไหม - *can [you], no?*): "kun àan jòt-mǎai níi dâi maǎi"... *you read letter this, can you?*

A reply to a *mǎi* question is made by repeating the verb if the answer is 'yes', or using ไม่ + **the verb** if the answer is 'no'. Pancake literally replies, "*I read cannot,*" (pǒm àan mâi dâi).

Consonant Sound: /k/

4th Letter of the Alphabet Kɔɔ Kwaai

ค

"สวัสดีค่ะ แพนเค้ก คุณอ่านจดหมายนี้ได้ไหม"
"Hello Pancake, can you read this?"

"เสียใจครับ ผมอ่านไม่ได้"
"Sorry, no."

"ผู้หญิงที่บ้านนั้นอาจจะอ่านได้"
"Perhaps the woman at the house?"

"เป็นความคิดที่ดี ขอบคุณค่ะ"
"A good idea, thank you."

ค

โค้ง (kóong – *bend, bow*); คือ (kʉʉ – *[to] be*); เคย (kəəi – *used to*)

ฅ

 ฅ คน　　　　　　Person

"อา-หาร กลิ่น น่า กิน ค่ะ คุณ แม่"
"aa-hǎan glìn nâa gin kâ kun mɛ̂ɛ"

"แม่ เห็น-ด้วย"
"mɛ̂ɛ hěn-dûai"

"เรียก ทุก-คน มา ทาน อา-หาร เที่ยง ได้ แล้ว"
"rîiak túk-kon maa taan aa-hǎan tîiang dâi lɛ́ɛo"

Thai Culture - Respect

Showing respect is a huge cultural element of Thai life. Conversely, not showing respect will mark you as someone who either doesn't know or simply rude.

This respect can be from simple things like taking your shoes off before you enter someone's home, to how you address another person, or the way you dress.

We will cover some of these to ensure you get the most out of your time in the LOS.

This Consonant is Obsolete.

5th Letter of the Alphabet ค ค Kon

ฆ

🔔 ฆ ระฆัง   Bell

"คุณ พ่อ คะ, พี่ คะ, อา-หาร พร้อม แล้ว ค่ะ"

"kun pɔ̂ɔ ká, pîi ká, aa-hǎan prɔ́ɔm lɛ́ɛɔ kâ"

Thai Culture - The Head and the Feet

The head is the highest point on the body and Thai's believe it to be spiritually above everything else. *Never* touch anyone on the head without asking their permission first, this also applies to children.

It is also considered rude to pass in the space above someone's head if they are sitting or kneeling.

You will see Thai people bow or crouch as they walk past you if you are sitting, this is to show respect. It would be very polite of you to do the same if you find yourself in a similar situation.

Consonant Sound: /k/

6th Letter of the Alphabet   Kɔɔ Rá-kang

"คุณพ่อคะ พี่คะ อาหารพร้อมแล้วค่ะ"
"Father, brother, food is ready."

Thai Culture - The Head and the Feet

The feet are the lowest part and are considered dirty. *Always* take your shoes off when entering someone's home. Never point your feet at other people and always walk around another's outstretched legs.

All Thai currency has His Majesty the King's portrait on it, if you drop a note, *never* step on it!

ฆ-รา-วาส (ká-raa-wâat – *buddhist layperson*)

ง

ง งู

Snake

[หาว] "หิว มาก"
[Hăao] "hĭo mâak"

"ไอ-ยา-รา อยู่ ที่ ไหน, เขา จะ ต้อง หิว แน่ นอน"
"Ai-yaa-raa yùu tîi năi, kăo jà dtɔ̂ɔng hĭo nɛ̂ɛ nɔɔn"

Thai Culture - Nicknames

For a westerner, Thai names can be a little bit difficult to get your tongue around. Fortunately, just about every Thai person has a nickname (*chûu-lêen*, ชื่อ-เล่น).

This is given to them by their parents at birth and is used throughout their life.

Consonant Sound: /ng/

7th Letter of the Alphabet   Ngɔɔ Nguu

[หาว] "หิวมาก"
[Yawn] "I'm very hungry!"

"ไอยาราอยู่ที่ไหน เขาจะต้องหิวแน่นอน"
"Where is Aiyarah, he'll be hungry."

Some of these nicknames can be humorous to foreigners but these are just friendly names. The fact that the person's name translates as chicken, frog or duck may give you a chuckle but you'll get over it.

Increasingly, due to Western influences, more and more Thais are being given English names.

ง่าย (ngâai – *easy*); เงิน (ngəən – *money*); แกง (gɛɛng – *curry*)

 จ จาน   Plate

"กิน กัน เถอะ"
"gin gan tò"

"ลูก-ชาย, ดน-ตรี โรง-เรียน ของ ลูก กี่ โมง"
"lûuk-chaai, don-dtrii roong-riian kɔ̌ɔng lûuk gìi moong"

"บ่าย 2 โมง ตรง ครับ"
"bàai sɔ̌ɔng moong dtrong kráp"

Thai Family Terms
- ผู้-ชาย (pûu-chaai - man)
- ผู้-หญิง (pûu-yǐng - woman)
- ผู้-ใหญ่ (pûu-yài - adult)
- เด็ก (dèk – child)
- ลูก-ชาย (lûuk-chaai - son)
- ลูก-สาว (lûuk-sǎao - daughter)
- สา-มี (sǎa-mii - husband)
- ภรร-ยา (pan-rá-yaa - wife)
- พ่อ (pɔ̂ɔ - father)
- แม่ (mɛ̂ɛ - mother)

Initial Consonant Sound: /j/ Final Consonant Sound: /t/

8th Letter of the Alphabet

Jɔɔ Jaan

"กิน กันเถอะ"
"Let's eat."

"ลูกชาย,ดนตรีโรงเรียนของลูก กี่โมง"
"Son, what time is your school concert?"

"บ่าย 2 โมงตรงครับ"
"At 2 p.m"

Thai Family Terms (continued)

- ผัว (pǔa - husband (informal))
- เมีย (miia - wife (informal))
- พี่-น้อง (pîi-nɔ́ɔng - relative)
- พี่-ชาย (pîi-chaai - older brother)
- พี่-สาว (pîi-sǎao - older sister)
- น้อง-ชาย (nɔ́ɔng-chaai - younger brother)
- น้อง-สาว (nɔ́ɔng-sǎao - younger sister)
- ปู่ (bpùu - father's father)
- ย่า (yâa - father's mother)
- more to follow...

จะ (jà – *will*, *shall*); จริง (jing – *really*, *true*); จาก (jàak – *from*); ใจ (jai – *heart*)

ฉ

 ฉ ฉิ่ง   Cymbals

"ปี ที่ แล้ว เดิน ข-บวน ส-นุก มาก ครับ"
"bpii tîi léɛo dəən kà-buan sà-nùk mâak kráp"

"พ่อ คิด ว่า วัน-นี้ ฝน จะ ตก"
"pɔ̂ɔ kít wâa wan-níi fŏn jà dtòk"

"แม่ จะ เอา ร่ม ไป ด้วย"
"mɛ̂ɛ jà ao rôm bpai dûai"

Thai Family Terms (contd)
- ตา (dtaa - mother's father)
- ยาย (yaai - mother's mother)
- ลุง (lung - father/mother's older brother)
- ป้า (bpâa - father/mother's older sister)
- น้า (náa - mother's younger brother or sister)
- อา (aa - father's younger brother or sister).

Initial Consonant Sound: /ch/ Final Consonant Sound: /t/

9th Letter of the Alphabet Chǒ:o Chìng

"ปีที่แล้วเดินขบวนสนุกมากครับ"

"The parade was fun last year."

"พ่อคิดว่าวันนี้ฝนจะตก"

"I think it will rain today."

"แม่จะเอาร่มไปด้วย"

"I will take an umbrella."

Note: the actual cymbals denoted by the Thai word 'chìng' are only small, They have been enlarged here for illustrative purposes.

ฉ

ฉัน (chǎn – [female]: *I, me* (informal)); **ฉ-ลาด** (chà-làat – *clever*)

ช

 ช ช้าง   Elephant

"ส-วัส-ดี ครับ ไอ-ยา-รา, ไป กิน อา-หาร เที่ยง กัน-เถอะ"
"sà-wàt-dii kráp ai-yaa-raa, bpai gin aa-hǎan tîiang gan-tè"

"ผม ไป ไม่ ได้"
"pǒm bpai mâi dâi!"

"ทำ-ไม ไม่ ได้"
"tam-mai mâi dâi"

Thai Culture - the Wai

The Wai is used to greet and show respect to people. This is where one's hands are joined as if in prayer and then a bow of the head is given to the person you are greeting or showing respect to.

The height of the hands and the depth of the bow indicate one's social status in reference to the other person, i.e. the person of lower social standing will Wai first, their hands will be positioned higher and their bow will be deeper than the reciprocated Wai.

Initial Consonant Sound: /ch/ Final Consonant Sound: /t/

10th Letter of the Alphabet   Chɔɔ Cháang

"สวัสดีครับ ไอยารา ไปกินอาหารเที่ยงกันเถอะ"
"Hello Aiyarah, let's go to lunch."

"ผมไปไม่ได้"
"I can't!"

"ทำไมไม่ได้"
"Why not?"

You must always show respect and Wai with your hands 'high' to monks and it shows great respect to Wai to older Thai people.

You should never Wai to service people such as waiters or bar staff.

There are 5 levels/heights of Wai but if, initially, you Wai with your fingertips touching the tip of your nose you won't go far wrong.

ช

ใช่ (châi – *yes, agree*); ชา (chaa – *tea*); ชาย (chaai – *male*); ใช้ (chái – *use*)

ซ  ซ โซ่   Chain

ซ โซ่   Chain

"เพราะ-ว่า โซ่ นี่"
"prɔ́-wâa sôo nîi"

"นี่ คือ ปัญ-หา"
"nîi kɯɯ bpan-hǎa"

"ให้ ผม คิด ดู ก่อน"
"hâi pǒm kít duu gɔ̀ɔn"

"ผม รู้ แล้ว"
"pǒm rúu lέεo"

Initial Consonant Sound: **/s/** Final Consonant Sound: **/t/**

11th Letter of the Alphabet   Sɔɔ Sôo

"เพราะว่าโซ่นี่"
"Because of this chain."

"นี่คือปัญหา"
"This is a problem!"

"ให้ผมคิดดูก่อน"
"Let me think."

"ผมรู้แล้ว"
"I know!"

ซ้าย (sáai – *left*); ซื้อ (súʉ – *buy*)

ฌ

 ฌ เฌอ   Tree

"เอา งวง ทำ แบบ-นี้"
"ao nguang tam bɛ̀ɛp-níi"

"และ ดึง!!"
"lɛ́ dɯng!!"

"เย้...คุณ อยาก กิน อา-หาร ไทย หรือ อา-หาร จีน"
"yaay...kun yàak gin aa-hǎan tai rɯ̌ɯ aa-hǎan jiin"

Initial Consonant Sound: /**ch**/ Final Consonant Sound: /**t**/

12th Letter of the Alphabet   Chɔɔ Chəə

"เอางวงทำแบบนี้"

"Do this with your trunk…"

"และดึง!!"

"…and pull!!"

"เย้….คุณอยากกินอาหารไทยหรืออาหารจีน"

"Yaay…do you want Thai or Chinese food?"

Surin Elephant Festival

The elephant is held in great esteem in Thailand and the Surin Elephant Festival takes place on the third Saturday in November.

Here hundreds of elephants show their skills and play tug-o-war, football, dance and perform.

It is a great event, attended by people from all across the country and foreigners alike, and is well worth a visit.

ฌาน (chaan – *contemplation*, e.g. เข้า ฌาน (kâo chaan – *to meditate*))

ญ  ญ หญิง

Woman

13th Letter of the Alphabet Yɔɔ Yĭng

ญ

ฌ

 **ฎ ชฎา** — Head-dress

"ฉัน อยาก เป็น นาง-รำ"
"chăn yàak bpen naang-ram"

"หรือ ฉัน อาจ-จะ สา-มารถ ช่วย ปก-ป้อง ประ-เทศ ของ ฉัน"
"rɯ̌ʉ chăn àat-jà săa-mâat chûai bpòk-bpɔ̂ɔng bprà-têet kɔ̌ɔng chăn"

Thai Culture - the Royal Family

The King of Thailand, His Majesty King Bhumibol Adulyadej, is Thailand's longest reigning monarch and the worlds longest serving head of state.

His Majesty is respected and loved by Thais to the point of reverence. Always keep this in mind when in Thailand.

If you go to the cinema the Royal Anthem is played before each film: please stand and respect His Majesty the King at this time.

The National Anthem is played twice daily at 0800 and 1800 at which time everyone stops what they are doing, stand to attention and pay respect to the anthem.

Initial Consonant Sound: /**d**/ Final Consonant Sound: /**t**/

14th Letter of the Alphabet **Dɔɔ Chá-daa**

"ฉันอยากเป็นนางรำ"
"I would love to be a dancer."

"หรือฉันอาจจะสามารถช่วยปกป้องประเทศของฉัน"
"Or maybe I could help defend my country."

ฎ

ชฎา (chá-daa - *head-dress*); ฎี-กา (dii-gaa – *supreme court*)

 ฏ ปฏัก   Spear

"ฉัน ต้อง-การ เป็น นัก-รบ"
"chǎn dtɔ̂ɔng-gaan bpen nák-róp"

"และ เข้ม-แข็ง"
"lɛ́ kêem-kěng"

- Day - *wan* (วัน) / Night - *kʉʉn* (คืน)
- Today - *wan-níi* (วัน-นี้)
- Tomorrow - *prûng-níi* (พรุ่ง-นี้)
- After tomorrow - *má-rʉʉn-níi* (มะ-รืน-นี้)
- Yesterday - *mʉ̂ʉa-waan-níi* (เมื่อ-วาน-นี้)
- Before yesterday - *mʉ̂ʉa-waan-sʉʉn* (เมื่อ-วาน-ซืน)
- Week - *aa-tít* (อา-ทิตย์) or sàp-daa (สัป-ดาห์)
- Weekend - *sǎo aa-tít* (เสาร์ อา-ทิตย์)

Initial Consonant Sound: **/dt/** Final Consonant Sound: **/t/**

15th Letter of the Alphabet   **Dtɔɔ Bpà-dtàk**

"ฉันต้องการเป็นนักรบ"

"I want to be a warrior!"

"และเข้มแข็ง"

"and be strong."

Days of the Week
- Monday - *wan-jan* (วัน-จันทร์)
- Tuesday - *wan-ang-kaan* (วัน-อัง-คาร)
- Wednesday - *wan-pút* (วัน-พุธ)
- Thursday - *wan-pá-rú-hàt-sà-bɔɔ-dii* (วัน-พ-ฤ-หั-ส-บ-ดี)
- Friday - *wan-sùk* (วัน-ศุกร์)
- Saturday - *wan-sǎo* (วัน-เสาร์)
- Sunday - *wan-aa-tít* (วัน-อา-ทิตย์)

ป-ฏิ-บัติ (bpà-dtì-bàt – *perform*); ป-ฏิ-ทิน (bpà-dtì-tin – *calendar*)

  Pedestal

"ฉัน จะ นำ กอง-ทัพ"

"chǎn jà nam gɔɔng-táp..."

"และ ปราบ ศัต-รู ทั้ง-หมด"

"...lɛ́ bpràap sàt-dtruu táng-mòt"

Thai Culture - Muay Thai

Most people have heard of Muay Thai, or Thai boxing. It is the traditional martial art in Thailand and most towns and cities will host competitions on a regular basis.

Before the bout, the *Wâi kruu ram muai* ceremony (ไหว้ ครู รำ มวย), is performed in the ring. This is an ancient ritual where the combatants pay their respects to their teachers and elders.

On completion, their ceremonial headbands are removed and the first of up to five, 3-minute rounds commences.

Fists, knees, hands, elbows and feet may be used and any part of the body, except the groin, may be hit.

Points are scored for every hit and penalty points are deducted for violations.

The competition ends with either a physical or a technical knockout, by the referees decision, or in a draw.

Source: http://www.muaythai-fighting.com

Consonant Sound: /t/

16th Letter of the Alphabet · Tǒo Tǎan

ฐา-นะ (tǎa-ná - *status, position*); ฐาน-ทัพ (tǎan-táp – *military base/camp*)

 ฑ มณโฑ   Giant's Wife

"ให้ ปี-ศาจ ช่วย พวก-เรา"

"hâi bpii-sàat chûai pûak-rao"

"และ...เดี๋ยว-ก่อน, คุณ ไม่ ใช่ ปี-ศาจ"

"lɛ́...dǐiao-gɔ̀ɔn, kun mâi châi bpii-sàat?"

Thai Culture - The Story of Nang Montoo

In Thai literature, a fox resides with 4 Rɯɯ-sǐis (ฤๅ-ษี - *hermit sages*) who give the fox food.

One day, a serpent-demon (nâak (นาค)), who was once embarassed by the Rɯɯ-sǐis, releases her poison into some milk in an effort to kill the sages.

The fox sees this and as it can't speak it jumps into the milk to protect the Rɯɯ-sǐi's. The fox drinks the milk and dies.

In gratitude, Rɯɯ-sǐi uses his magic to transform the dead fox into a beautiful lady and then escorts her to an angel in heaven.

Later, as a prize for straightening a mountain, the angel gives Nang Montoo to a giant to become his beautiful wife.

Consonant Sound: /t/

17th Letter of the Alphabet   Tɔɔ Montoo

"ให้ปีศาจช่วยพวกเรา"
"Get demons to help us."

"และ...เดี๋ยวก่อนคุณไม่ใช่ปีศาจ"
"and...wait, you're not a demon?"

มณ-ฑล (mon-ton – *county*, *precinct*, *circle*)

ฅม ฅม ผู้เฒ่า   Elderly Man

"ทำ ใจ ให้ ส-งบ ลูก-สาว"

"tam jai hâi sà-ngòp lûuk-săao"

"ลูก กำ-ลัง ฝัน"

"lûuk gam-lang făn"

Thai Culture - Saving Face

Saving face is a huge factor in understanding Thai people and their culture.

Many are sensitive to this concept and Thai people are no exception: no one wants to be seen to lose face.

Very often an uncomfortable situation will be treated with a smile and the uttering of *mâi bpen rai* (ไม่ เป็น ไร): this often used phrase typifies Thai attitude and it basically means never mind, it'll be okay; somewhat similar to the French c'est la vie.

Consonant Sound: /t/

18th Letter of the Alphabet ฒ Tɔɔ Pûu-tâo

"ทำใจให้สงบลูกสาว"
"Calm yourself daughter."

"ลูกกำลังฝัน"
"You are just dreaming."

ฒ

ผู้ (pûu - *person*); เฒ่า (tâo - *elderly*, *old*); ผู้-เฒ่า (Pûu-tâo - *Elderly Man*)

ณ

ณ เณร — Monk

"ไม่ มี ความ-จำ-เป็น ที่ จะ สู้-รบ"

"mâi mii kwaam-jam-bpen tîi jà sûu-róp"

"คิด-ถึง กรรม ดี"

"kít-tɯ̆ɯng gam dii"

Thai Culture - Buddhism

Thailand is approximately 95% Therevada Buddhist and is strongly influenced by traditional beliefs regarding ancestral and natural spirits which have been incorporated into Buddhist cosmology.

Most Thai people own spirit houses, miniature wooden houses in which they believe household spirits live. They present offerings of food and drink to these spirits to keep them happy. If these spirits aren't happy, it is believed that they will inhabit the larger household of the Thai, and cause chaos. These spirit houses can be found in public places and in the streets of Thailand, where the public make offerings.

Source: www.en.wikipedia.org/wiki/Culture_of_Thailand

Consonant Sound: /n/

19th Letter of the Alphabet   Nɔɔ Neen

"ไม่มีความจำเป็นที่จะสู้รบ"

"There is no need to fight."

"คิดถึงกรรมดี"

"Think of good karma."

ณ-รงค์ (ná-rong - *fight*); ณ เว-ลา-นั้น (ná wee-laa-nán - *at that time*)

ด      ด เด็ก   Child

"คุณ แม่ คะ, ช่วย ด้วย"

"kun mɛ̂ɛ ká, chûai dûai"

"เป็น อะ-ไร, ลูก-สาว"

"bpen-à-rai, lûuk-săao"

"เขา ได้-รับ บาด เจ็บ ค่ะ"

"kăo dâi-ráp bàat jèp kâ"

Sànùk (สนุก) - to be fun, enjoyable

Everybody wants to have fun and, in Thailand, sà-nùk plays a major part in people's lives.

It means more than just to have fun, it is more of a concept, and transforms into meeting friends, eating out with friends, having fun at work, etc.

If you find yourself out with some Thai friends, you will probably be asked "Sà-nùk măi" (ส-นุก ไหม) ("*fun, nɔ́*?" or, "are you having fun?").

Initial Consonant Sound: /d/ Final Consonant Sound: /t/

20th Letter of the Alphabet   Dɔɔ Dèk

ดี (dii – *good, well*); ดู (duu – *look*); เดิน (dəən – *walk*); ได้ (dâi – *can, able*)

ต

  ต เต่า   Turtle

"ใคร เจ็บ"
"krai jèp"

"เต่า ตัว นี้ ค่ะ"
"dtào dtua níi kâ?"

"แม่ เข้า ใจ แล้ว"
"mɛ̂ɛ kâo jai lɛ́ɛo"

Thai Culture - Temples

Most temples have a dress code. This usually means shoulders must be covered and in some temples, long trousers are required.

You must always remove your shoes before you enter the sacred areas of a temple. You will see where to leave your shoes, they are quite safe.

When you sit or kneel within the temple, be careful not to point your feet at a Buddha image or anything that is sacred, tuck your feet away.

Initial Consonant Sound: /**dt**/ Final Consonant Sound: /**t**/

21st Letter of the Alphabet   **Dtɔɔ Dtào**

"ใครเจ็บ"
"Who's hurt?"

"เต่าตัวนี้ค่ะ"
"This turtle."

"แม่เข้าใจแล้ว"
"I see."

Photography is permitted within temples unless
signs say otherwise.

Before you begin taking photographs, please show
respect to the temple, to Buddha and to a monk if
one is present. I have seen too many tourists enter
a temple and just start clicking away!

It is also polite to show respect as you leave.

แต่ (dtɛ̀ɛ – *but, since*); ต-ลก (dtà-lòk – *funny*)

ถ

 ถ ถุง   Bag

Tǒo Tǔng

ถ

ถึง (tǔng - *reach, arrive*); ถูก (tùuk – *cheap, correct*); ถาม (tǎam – *ask*)

ท

ท ทหาร   Soldier

23rd Letter of the Alphabet   ทอ Táhǎan

ไท (tai – *freedom, independence*); ทอด (tɔ̂ɔd – *deep-fried*); ทำ-ไม (tam-mai – *why*)

ธ

 ธ ธง   Flag

24th Letter of the Alphabet ธอ Tong

ธ

ธ

ธรรม (tham – *dharma, religious teaching/duty*)

น

  น หนู Mouse

"เช้า นี้ ยุ่ง มาก!"
"cháo níi yûng maak"

"ผม ต้อง ไป พบ เพื่อน ของ ผม"
"pǒm dtɔ̂ɔng bpai póp pʉ̂ʉan kɔ̌ɔng pǒm"

"ผม จะ ใช้ ใบ ไหน ดี"
"pǒm jà chái bai nǎi dii"

Thai Culture - Monks

Monks have a special status in Thailand and are respected throughout society.

Monks and laymen follow the *Vinaya* - prá-wí-nai (พระ-วิ-นัย). This is the framework for the education and discipline for Buddhism.

At the core of the *Vinaya* are the rules known as *Precepts*. These are the directives that monks live their lives by and will lead them to greater wisdow. There are different levels of Precepts, 5 for the majority of buddhists, 8 and 10 for laymen and 227 Precepts for ordained monks, or Bhikkus (pík-kù, ภิก-ขุ).

Source: http://siamfoundation.org/thailand-faq/index.php?action=artikel&cat=5&id=3&artlang=en

Consonant Sound: /n/

25th Letter of the Alphabet   Nɔɔ Nǔn

"เช้านี้ยุ่งมาก!"
"It's very busy this morning."

"ผมต้องไปพบเพื่อนของผม"
"I have to go and meet my friend."

"ผมจะใช้ใบไหนดี"
"Which one shall I use?"

น ม (nom – *milk*); นก (nók – *bird*); นั้น (nán – *that*); นั่ง (nâng – *sit*)

บ

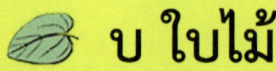 บ ใบไม้   Leaf

"วัน-นี้ อา-กาศ ดี"
"wan-níi aa-gàat dii"

"จะ ใช้ ใบ นี้"
"jà chái bai níi"

"โอ-เว่น อยู่ ที่-ไหน"
"Oo-wêen yùu tîi-nǎi"

Thai Culture - Religious Merit

Many Thai's support monks with donations of food and other similar acts of aid. This brings them religious merit or bun (บุญ) which will assist them in this and in the next life.

If you got to a temple and a monk wants to practice his English then it is okay to talk to him.

Remember, always keep your head lower than his and if you wish to give him something, place it on the ground in front of him.

Women must never touch a monk or a monk's robe and must never sit next to a monk unless it is at a lower level.

Initial Consonant Sound: /**b**/ Final Consonant Sound: /**p**/

"วันนี้อากาศดี"
"It is a beautiful day."

"จะใช้ใบนี้"
"This one will do."

"โอเว่น อยู่ที่ไหน"
"Where is Owain?"

บ้าน (bâan – *house*, *home*); พบ (póp – *meet*, *find*)

ป

ป ปลา

Fish

ป

"สวัสดีครับ เอลโม่ คุณได้ลูกกวาดของผมไหม"
"Hello Elmo, did you get my candy?"

"ครับ นี่ไง"
"Yes, here it is."

"ขอบคุณครับ เอลโม่ เจอกันพรุ่งนี้ครับ"
"Thank you Elmo, see you tomorrow?"

"ตกลงครับ"
"Okay."

ป

ไป (bpai – *go*); ปี (bpii – *year*); เปิด (bpə̀ət – *open*); ปิด (bpit – *close*)

ผ

 ผ ผึ้ง   Bee

"พวก-เขา อยู่ ที่ ไหน"
"pûak-kăo yùu tîi năi"

"พวก-เขา อยู่ ที่-นี่ ที่-ใด ที่-หนึ่ง"
"pûak-kăo yùu tîi-nîi tîi-dai tîi-nùng"

Thai Culture - Buddhist Precepts

The **Five Precepts** are the basic guidelines for all buddhists:

1. To refrain from destroying living creatures
2. To refrain from stealing
3. To refrain from adulterous, or wrong sexual activity
4. To refrain from lying, slanderous or harmful speech
5. To refrain from intoxicating drinks and drugs which lead to carelessness.

Remember, these are guidelines, not rules and not everyone sticks to them.

Source: http://siamfoundation.org/thailand-faq/index.php?action=artikel&cat=5&id=3&artlang=en

Consonant Sound: /p/

28th letter of the Alphabet

Pɔ̌ɔ Pûng

"พวกเขาอยู่ที่ไหน"
"Where are they?"

"พวกเขาอยู่ที่นี่ที่ใดที่หนึ่ง"
"They are here somewhere."

10 Precepts:

6. To refrain from eating after mid-day

7. To refrain from dancing, singing, music, going to see entertainments,

8. To refrain from wearing garlands, using perfumes, and beautifying the body with cosmetics

9. To refrain from lying on a high or luxurious sleeping place

10. To refrain from accepting gold and silver (money).

ผิด (pìt – *wrong, incorrect*); ผ่าน (pàan – *cross, pass*); แผ่น (pɛ̀ɛn – *sheet, plank*)

ฝ

 ฝ ฝา   Lid

"พวก-เขา อยู่ ที่-นั่น"
"pûak-kǎo yùu tîi-nân"

"งาน-เลี้ยง ได้ เริ่ม แล้ว"
"ngaan-líiang dâi rêəm lέεo"

"ฝา สวย!"
"fǎa sǔai"

Months of the Year

January - má-gà-raa-kom (ม-ก-รา-คม)   July - gà-rá-gà-daa-kom (ก-ร-ก-ฎา-คม)

February - gum-paa-pan (กุม-ภา-พันธ์)   August - sǐng-hǎa-kom (สิง-หา-คม)

March - mii-naa-kom (มี-นา-คม)   September - gan-yaa-yon (กัน-ยา-ยน)

April - mee-sǎa-yon (เม-ษา-ยน)   October - dtù-laa-kom (ตุ-ลา-คม)

May - prút-sà-paa-kom (พฤ-ษ-ภา-คม)   November - prút-sà-ji-gaa-yon (พฤ-ศ-จิ-กา-ยน)

June - mí-tù-naa-yon (มิ-ถุ-นา-ยน)   December - tan-waa-kom (ธัน-วา-คม)

Initial Consonant Sound: /f/ Final Consonant Sound: /p/

ฝน (fǒn – *rain*); ฝรั่ง (fà-ràng – *non-Asian foreigner*); ฝัน (fǎn – *dream*)

พ

  พ พาน Tray

"ผม รู้-สึก กระ-หาย"
"pŏm rúu-sùk grà-hăai"

"ผม อยาก ดื่ม เบียร์ สัก ขวด"
"pŏm yàak dùum biia sàk kùat"

"ฟี-บี้ อยาก ดื่ม ไวน์ แดง สัก แก้ว"
"Fee-bêe yàak dùum wai dɛɛng sàk gɛ̂ɛo"

Consonant Sound: /p/

30th Letter of the Alphabet　　　Pɔɔ Paan

พ่อ (pɔ̂ɔ - *father*); พัน (pan - *1,000*); พี่ (pîi - *older sibling*); เพิ่ง (pə̂əng - *just now, recent*)

ฟ

 ฟ ฟัน   Tooth

"อา-หาร เย็น อ-ร่อย มาก"
"aa-hǎan yen à-rɔ̀ɔi mâak"

"ส้ม-ตำ คือ อา-หาร โปรด ของ ผม"
"sôm-dtam kɯɯ aa-hǎan bpròot kɔ̌ɔng pǒm"

"ผม ต้อง-การ น้ำ-ผึ้ง"
"pǒm dtɔ̂ɔng-gaan nám-pɯ̂ng"

Eating Out

In Thailand, eating out with friends is a popular occurrence and a great social occasion: it is all part of the concept of *sà-nùk* (สนุก).

When you sit to eat, there is no starter and main course, everybody orders and the food is set down for all to enjoy.

The waiter or waitress will serve you your plate with just rice or in a bowl.

Initial Consonant Sound: **/f/** Final Consonant Sound: **/p/**

31st Letter of the Alphabet　　Fɔɔ Fan　　ฟ

"อาหารเย็นอร่อยมาก"
"Dinner was very delicious."

"ส้มตำ คือ อาหารโปรดของผม"
"Somtam is my favourite."

"ผมต้องการน้ำผึ้ง"
"I want honey!"

Use the serving spoon with each dish to bring food to your plate, no more than one or two spoonfulls at a time and then savour the delcious textures, flavours and spices with cooked rice (kâao sŭai, ข้าว สวย).

ฟ

ไฟ (fai – *fire, flame*); ฟ้า (fáa – *sky*); ฟัง (fang – *listen*)

ภ  ภ สำเภา   Junk

"ผม ชอบ เรือ ลำ นั้น"
"pŏm chɔ̂ɔp rɯɯa lam nán"

"ช้าๆ หน่อย"
"cháa cháa nɔ̀ɔi"

"ขอ-โทษ ครับ"
"kɔ̌ɔ-tôot kráp"

Songkran

The three day Songkran festival (Sŏng-graan - สง-กรานต์) marks the start of the Thai New Year. It runs from 13-15th April and is a national holiday.

The festival involves sprinkling water onto holy images in order to cleanse and in hope that it will bring good luck and prosperity in the forthcoming year.

Consonant Sound: /p/

32nd Letter of the Alphabet   Pɔɔ Sămpao

"ผมชอบเรือลำนั้น"
"I like that boat."

"ช้าๆ หน่อย"
"Slow down!"

"ขอโทษครับ"
"Sorry."

Nowadays, for a lot of people, the emphasis is more towards partying, soaking people and covering them in chalk (*din-rŏ̌ɔ-pɔɔng* - ดิน-สอ-พอง).

ภา-ษา (paa-săa – *language, speech, words*); ภาพ (pâap – *picture, drawing*)

ม

ม ม้า   Horse

"ผมหวังว่า ผมจะมีเรือแบบนั้น"
"I wish I had a boat like that."

"นี่คืองานหนัก"
"This is hard work."

"มันคงจะง่ายขึ้น ถ้า..."
"It would be much easier if..."

ม

มาก (mâak – *much, many*); ไม่ (mâi – *no, not*); เมีย (miia – *wife*); แม่ (mɛ̂ɛ - *mother*)

ย

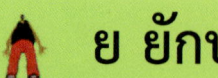 **ย ยักษ์**   Giant

"...ยักษ์ ช่วย ผม"
"...yák chûai pǒm"

"จาก-นั้น ผม คง-จะ ดึง เรือ นี้ อย่าง ง่าย ๆ"
"jàak-nán pǒm kong-jà dɯng rɯɯa níi yàang ngâai ngâai"

Initial Consonant Sound: /y/ Final Consonant Sound: /i/

34th Letter of the Alphabet   Yɔɔ Yák

ยักษ์ช่วยผม"
"...a giant helped me!"

"จากนั้น ผมคงจะดึงเรือนี้อย่างง่าย ๆ"
"Then I could pull this boat easily."

ยาก (yâak – *hard, difficult*); ยัง (yang – *yet, still*); แยก (yɛ̂ɛk - *intersection*)

ร

 ร เรือ　　　　　　　Boat

Initial Consonant Sound: /r/ Final Consonant Sound: /n/

Rɔɔ Rʉʉa    ร

ร

เร็ว (reo – *fast, quick*); รำ (ram – *dance*); เรียก (rîiak – *call*)

ล

 ล ลิง — Monkey

"นั่น อะ-ไร อยู่ บน พื้น"
"nân à-rai yùu bon pᴚᴚn"

"ผม จะ ไป ดู"
"pŏm jà bpai duu"

Initial Consonant Sound: /l/ Final Consonant Sound: /n/

36th Letter of the Alphabet   ลวว Ling

"นั่นอะไรอยู่บนพื้น"
"What is that on the floor?"

"ผมจะไปดู"
"I will go and have a look."

และ (lɛ́ - *and*); ลืม (lɯɯm – *forget*); เล่น (lêen – *play*, *have fun*, *amuse*); เลว (leeo - *bad*)

ว

ว แหวน   Ring

Initial Consonant Sound: /w/ Final Consonant Sound: /o/

37th Letter of the Alphabet Wɔɔ Wĕɛ ŋ ว

"สวยมาก"
"It's very beautiful."

"ผมสงสัยว่ามันเป็นของใคร"
"I wonder who it belongs to?"

"ผมจะเอามันไปหาฤๅษี"
"I'll take it to Rʉʉ-sĭi."

"ท่านจะต้องรู้ว่าทำอย่างไร"
"He will know what to do."

ว

วัน (wan – *day*); วิ่ง (wîng – *run*); เวลา (wee-laa – *time*); วัด (wât - *temple*, *measure*)

 ศ ศาลา   Tent/Pavilion

"ท่าน อยู่ นั่น"
"tâan yùu nân"

Initial Consonant Sound: /s/ Final Consonant Sound: /t/

38th Letter of the Alphabet   Sŏ̌ɔ Sǎa-laa

ศูนย์ (sǔun – *zero, 0*); ศาล (sǎan – *court*); วัน ศุกร์ (wan sùk – *Friday*)

ษ

 ษ ฤๅษี Hermit

"ขอ-โทษ ครับ ท่าน ฤๅ-ษี"
"kɔ̌ɔ-tôot kráp tâan rɯɯ-sǐi"

"มี อะ-ไร ให้ ช่วย ไหม"
"mii à-rai hâi chûai mǎi"

"ผม เก็บ แหวน นี้ ได้ และ อยาก คืน มัน ให้ เจ้า-ของ ครับ"
"pǒm gèp wɛ̌ɛn níi dâi lɛ́ yàak kɯɯn man hâi jâo-kɔ̌ɔng kráp"

"ทิ้ง มัน ไว้ ที่-นี่ เจ้า-ของ มัน จะ มา รับ คืน"
"tíng man wái tîi-nîi jâo-kɔ̌ɔng man jà maa ráp kɯɯn"

Initial Consonant Sound: /s/ Final Consonant Sound: /t/

39th Letter of the Alphabet

ฤๅ Rʉʉ-sǐi

"ขอโทษครับ ท่านฤๅษี"
"Excuse me rʉʉ-sǐi?"

มีอะไรให้ช่วยไหม"
"How can I help you."

"ผมเก็บแหวนนี้ได้และอยากคืนมันให้เจ้าของครับ"
"I have found this beautiful ring and want to return it to its owner."

"ทิ้งมันไว้ที่นี่เจ้าของมันจะมารับคืน"
"Leave it here, its owner will receive it. "

ส  ส เสือ   Tiger

"เป็น อะ-ไร"
"bpen à-rai"

"ผม เป็น-หวัด และ มี-ไข้ ครับ"
"pǒm bpen-wàt lɛ́ mii-kâi kráp"

"ช่วย ผม ได้ ไหม ครับ"
"chûai pǒm dâi mǎi kráp"

"ได้"
"dâi"

Initial Consonant Sound: /s/ Final Consonant Sound: /t/

รว๊ว รัหล    ส

"เป็นอะไร"
"What is wrong?"

"ผมเป็นหวัดและมีไข้ครับ"
"I have a cold and fever."

"ช่วยผมได้ไหมครับ"
"Can you help me?"

"ได้"
"Yes, I can."

ส

สิง-โต (sĭng dto – *lion*); ส-นุก (sà-nùk – *fun, enjoyable*); ใส่ (sài – *add, put in*)

ห

  ห หีบ   Chest

Consonant Sound: /h/ (Can also be a silent consonant: /-/)

Hǒɔ Hìip

"นี่คือของขวัญ"
"Here are some gifts."

หก (hòk - *six, ๖*); หนัง (nǎng - *movie, leather*); หมด (mòt - *empty, finish*)

ศ

 ศ จุฬา

Star-shaped Kite

"ระ-วัง ข้าง-นอก ลม-แรง"

"rá-wang kâang-nɔ̂ɔk lom-rɛɛng"

Initial Consonant Sound: /l/ Final Consonant Sound: /n/

42nd Letter of the Alphabet   เฬ Jù-laa

"ระวัง ข้างนอกลมแรง"

"Be careful, it is windy out there."

ฬ

ฬ

จุฬา (jù-laa – *star* or *bird shaped kite*)

อ

 อ อ่าง   Bowl

43rd Letter of the Alphabet วว Àang

"สูดควันเข้าลึก ๆ"
"Breathe the fumes deeply."

"ไข้จะลดลง"
"Your fever will abate."

อัง-กฤษ (ang-grìt - *English*); อีก (ìik - *again*); อยู่ (yùu – *[to be] somewhere (location)*)

ฮ

 ฮ นกฮูก   Owl

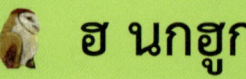

"ส-วัส-ดี ตอน-เช้า ครับ"
"sà-wàt-dii dtɔɔn-cháo kráp"

"ใน ป่า เงียบ มาก"
"nai bpàa ngîap màak"

"ผม สง-สัย ว่า เกิด อะไร ขึ้น บ้าง วัน-นี้"
"pǒm sǒng-sǎi wâa gèət à-rai kɐ̂n bâang wan-níi"

Consonant Sound: /h/

44th Letter of the Alphabet   Hɔɔ Nók-hûuk

"สวัสดีตอนเช้าครับ"
"Good morning."

"ในป่าเงียบมาก"
"The jungle is very quiet."

"ผมสงสัยว่าเกิดอะไรขึ้นบ้างวันนี้"
"I wonder what's been happening today?"

ฮึก-เหิม (húk-hə̌əm - arrogant, conceited); ฮ่อง กง (*Hɔ̀ɔng Kong - Hong Kong*)

Appendices

Appendix A. Initial and Final Consonant Sounds

The table below shows a complete list of consonants colour coded by consonant class, their initial and their final consonant sounds:

Table A.1 - Initial and Final Consonant Sounds

No.	Thai Character	Transliterated Text Name	Meaning	Initial Consonant Sound	Final Consonant Sound
1	ก ไก่	Gɔɔ Gài	Chicken	/g/	/k/
2	ข ไข่	Kɔ̌ɔ Kài	Egg	/k/	
3	ฃ ขวด	Kɔ̌ɔ Kùat	Bottle	Obsolete	
4	ค ควาย	Kɔɔ Kwaai	Buffalo	/k/	
5	ฅ คน	Kɔɔ Kon	Person	Obsolete	
6	ฆ ระฆัง	Kɔɔ Rá-kang	Bell	/k/	
7	ง งู	Ngɔɔ Nguu	Snake	/ng/	
8	จ จาน	Jɔɔ Jaan	Plate	/j/	/t/
9	ฉ ฉิ่ง	Chɔ̌ɔ Chìng	Cymbals	/ch/	/t/
10	ช ช้าง	Chɔɔ Cháang	Elephant	/ch/	/t/
11	ซ โซ่	Sɔɔ Sôo	Chain	/s/	/t/
12	ฌ เฌอ	Chɔɔ Chəə	Tree	/ch/	/t/
13	ญ หญิง	Yɔɔ Yǐng	Woman	/y/	/n/
14	ฎ ชฎา	Dɔɔ Chá-daa	Head-dress	/d/	/t/
15	ฏ ปฏัก	Dtɔɔ Bpà-dtàk	Spear	/dt/	/t/
16	ฐ ฐาน	Tɔ̌ɔ Tǎan	Pedestal	/t/	
17	ฑ มณโท	Tɔɔ Montoo	Giant's Wife	/t/	
18	ฒ ผู้เฒ่า	Tɔɔ Pûu-tâo	Old Man	/t/	
19	ณ เณร	Nɔɔ Neen	Monk	/n/	
20	ด เด็ก	Dɔɔ Dèk	Child	/d/	/t/

Table A.1 - Initial and Final Consonant Sounds

21	ต เต่า	Dtɔɔ Dtào	Turtle	/dt/	/t/
22	ถ ถุง	Tɔ̌ɔ Tǔng	Bag	/t/	
23	ท ทหาร	Tɔɔ Tá-hǎan	Soldier	/t/	
24	ธ ธง	Tɔɔ Tong	Flag	/t/	
25	น หนู	Nɔɔ Nǔu	Mouse	/n/	
26	บ ใบไม้	Bɔɔ Bai-mái	Leaf	/b/	/p/
27	ป ปลา	Bpɔɔ Bplaa	Fish	/bp/	/p/
28	ผ ผึ้ง	Pɔ̌ɔ Pɯ̂ng	Bee	/p/	
29	ฝ ฝา	Fɔ̌ɔ Fǎa	Lid	/f/	/p/
30	พ พาน	Pɔɔ Paan	Tray	/p/	
31	ฟ ฟัน	Fɔɔ Fan	Tooth	/f/	/p/
32	ภ สำเภา	Pɔɔ Sǎmpao	Junk	/p/	
33	ม ม้า	Mɔɔ Máa	Horse	/m/	
34	ย ยักษ์	Yɔɔ Yák	Giant	/y/	/i/
35	ร เรือ	Rɔɔ Rɯɯa	Boat	/r/	/n/
36	ล ลิง	Lɔɔ Ling	Monkey	/l/	/n/
37	ว แหวน	Wɔɔ Wɛ̌ɛn	Ring	/w/	/o/
38	ศ ศาลา	Sɔ̌ɔ Sǎa-laa	Tent	/s/	/t/
39	ษ ฤษี	Sɔ̌ɔ Rɯɯ-sǐi	Hermit	/s/	/t/
40	ส เสือ	Sɔ̌ɔ Sɯ̌ɯa	Tiger	/s/	/t/
41	ห หีบ	Hɔ̌ɔ Hìip	Chest	/h/	
42	ฬ จุฬา	Lɔɔ Jù-laa	Star-shaped Kite	/l/	/n/
43	อ อ่าง	ɔɔ Àang	Bowl	/ɔɔ/	
44	ฮ นกฮูก	Hɔɔ Nók-hûuk	Owl	/h/	

Appendix B. Summary of the Alphabet Story

The following list is a summary of the entire 44 consonant story. Learning this will help to recall the story, remind you of the individual consonant names and the sequence of the alphabet.

1. Millie (มิลลี่), the <u>chicken</u>, says hello.

2. Millie goes to meet her <u>egg</u>-friend Pollo (พอลโล่), who has found a bottle.

3. They try to read the message (in a <u>bottle</u>). They can't, so they ask Pancake.

4. They ask Pancake (แพนเค้ก) the <u>water buffalo</u> if he can read it; he can't so suggests asking the woman in the house.

5. Mother (<u>person</u>) is cooking lunch for her daughter.

6. The daughter rings the <u>bell</u> for food.

7. This wakes Ashara (อาชารา) the <u>snake</u> who goes to find Aiyarah.

8. The family sits for dinner and mother passes the <u>plates</u>.

9. The son gets his <u>cymbals</u> for the school parade.

10. Ashara finds Aiyarah (ไอยารา) the <u>elephant</u>.

11. Aiyarah is attached to the tree with a <u>chain</u>.

12. Aiyarah and Ashara, pull the <u>tree</u> out.

13. <u>Woman</u> rests in a clearing and falls asleep. She then starts to dream.

14. Perhaps she will be a famous dancer (dons her <u>head-dress</u>).

15. Then she picks up a <u>spear</u>.

16. Whilst standing on a <u>pedestal</u>, she addresses her army.

17. She then tries to summon a demon but Nang Montoo, the <u>giant's wife</u>, appears to calm her down.

18. Then her father, now an <u>elderly man</u>, appears in her dream.

19. Finally, a young <u>monk</u> talks to her through her dream.

20. Then she is woken by her <u>child</u>, who needs help.

21. They see a wounded <u>turtle</u>.

22. She has medicine in her <u>bag</u> and helps the turtle.

23. A company of <u>soldiers</u> marches past...

24. ...carrying their Thai <u>flag</u>.

25. A <u>mouse</u> (Elmo - เอลโม่) watches this from the river bank...

26. ...and gets on a <u>leaf</u> to go and see his friend.

27. Owain (โอเว่น - a <u>fish</u>) stops to talk to Elmo.

28. A <u>bee</u> flies overhead, looking for the party.

29. He sees the party on a floating <u>lid</u>.

30. More bees arrive carrying food and drink on <u>trays</u>.

31. One big fat bee with a very sweet <u>tooth</u>.

32. <u>Yacht</u> sails by almost upsetting the party.

33. A tired <u>horse</u> (Apache - อาปาชี่) is dreaming.

34. Apache dreams of a <u>giant</u> coming to aid him.

35. Then it's back to reality and Apache continues to pull the <u>boat</u> up the river.

36. Moxie (มกซี่ - a <u>monkey</u>) is looking down from the trees and sees something shiny on the floor.

37. He picks up the shiny <u>ring</u> and wants to return it to its owner.

38. Moxie goes to see the hermit at the <u>tent</u>.

39. Moxie and the <u>hermit</u> talk.

40. Qilin (ขิลิน - the <u>tiger</u>) arrives with a sore head.

41. The hermit looks into the <u>chest</u> to give them gifts.

42. He gives a <u>kite</u> to Moxie (to thank him for being honest).

43. ...and a <u>bowl</u> to Qilin, to steam away his fever.

44. As the sun sets, Jawhar (จอหาร์ - the <u>owl</u>) watches from the trees.

Jomtien beach

Appendix C. Other Language Notes

Here are some other features and aspects of Thai that you need to be aware of and understand.

Appendix C.1 Special Signs and Features

Additional signs that you will see in written Thai:

- ๆ (ไม้ ย-มก) - this is called **Mái Yá-mók** and it means that the previous word needs to be repeated, e.g. จริง ๆ (jing jing - meaning *real, true* or, in this case, *real real* or, *really?*).

Note: this word is pronounced /jing/ and not /jring/ as Rɔɔ Rʉʉa is silent here.

- The sign ฯ **Bpee-yaan-nɔ́ɔi** (เป-ยาล-น้อย) is used for abbreviation, e.g. กรุง-เทพ ฯ - *Grung-têep* (Bangkok).

  When you see this sign you have to pronounce the full word when speaking (if you know it). The full word for Bangkok is *Grung-têep-má-hăa-ná-kɔɔn* (กรุง-เทพ-ม-หา-น-คร).

- The sign ฯลฯ (เป-ยาล-ใหญ่) **Bpee-yaan-yài** is used in a similar manner to 'etc.' in English. When spoken, it is pronounced as /lá/ (ละ).
- The sign ์ (กา-รันต์) is called the **gaa-ran** and is used to make the letter it is above silent. It is most commonly seen in western words written in Thai.

  For example, the word beer - biia (เบียร์).

Appendix C.2 Sà-rà Ai Mái-Múan

Only 20 words in the Thai language use sà-rà ai mái-múan (ใ- /ai/), these are:

- ใช่ (châi - *yes*)
- ใช้ (chái - *use*)
- ใคร (krai - *who*)
- ใคร่ (krâi - *desire*)
- ใส (săi - *clear*)
- ใส่ (sài - *put in*)
- ใบ (bai - *leaf*)
- ใบ้ (bâi - *mute, dumb*)
- ใจ (jai - *heart*)
- ใด (dai - *any*)

- ใต้ (dtâi - *south, underneath*)
- ไฝ่ (fài - *aim*)
- ให้ (hâi - *give, let, permit*)
- ใหญ่ (yài - *big, large*)
- ใหม่ (mài - *new, again*)

- ใน (nai - *in*)
- ใย (yai - *web, fiber*)
- ใกล้ (glâi - *near, close*)
- สะใภ้ (sà-pái - *daughter in law*)
- หลง-ใหล (lŏng-lăi - *fascinating*)

Appendix C.3 Double ร (ร หัน - Rɔɔ Hǎn)

- You will sometimes see a double cluster of Rɔɔ Rʉʉa (รร) when reading Thai. This is called *Rɔɔ Hǎn* (ร หัน) and is either pronounced as /a/ when it is in the medial position in a syllable or as /an/ when in the final position. For example:

- มรรค (mák - *path*)
- สรรพ (sàp - *whole, all, entire*)
- สรร (sǎn - *choose*)
- บรรจุ (ban-jù - *load, fill*).

Appendix C.4 Consonant Clusters

Consonant clusters are groups of two consonants at the beginning of a syllable. Here are the five initial consonant sounds:

Table C.4.1 - Initial Consonants

Initial Consonant(s)	Sound
ก	/g/
ข and ค	/k/
ต	/dt/
ป	/bp/
ผ and พ	/p/

The second consonants will always be either ร (Rɔɔ Rʉʉa), ล (Lɔɔ Ling) or ว (Wɔɔ Wɛ̌ɛn).

The following table shows the complete list of consonant clusters:

Table C.4.2 - List of Consonant Clusters

Cluster	Pronunciation	Example
กร-	/gr/	โกรธ (gròot - *angry*)
กล-	/gl/	กลับ (glàp - *return, go back*)
กว-	/gw/	กว่า (gwàa - *more*)
ขร-	/kr/	ขรึม (krŭm - *serious*)
ขล-	/kl/	ขลุ่ย (klùi - flute)
ขว-	/kw/	ขวา (kwăa - *right*)
คร-	/kr/	ครับ (kráp - *polite particle used by males*)
คล-	/kl/	โคลง (kloong - *poem, poetry*)
คว-	/kw/	ความ (kwaam - *a prefix that converts a verb or an adjective into an abstract noun*)
ตร-	/dtr/	ตรง (dtrong - *at, straight*)
ปร-	/bpr/	ประ-เทศ (bprà-têet - *country, nation*)
ปล-	/bpl/	ปลา (bplaa - *fish*)
ผล-	/pl/	ผลัก (plàk - *push, shove*)
พร-	/pr/	พระ (prá - *buddha image or statue*)
พล-	/pl/	พลิก (plík - *turn over*)

Appendix C.5 Too & Roo

Too Tá-hăan (ท) does not form a consonant cluster. However, when the second consonant is *Roo Ruua* (ร) there are seventeen instances in Thai language where they form a <u>separate</u> sound of soo (/s/); this is from the consonant *soo sôo* (ซ).

This amalgamation can be written as: ท+ร = ซ or /t/+/r/ = /s/.

This may appear confusing but try and remember Too + Roo = Soo

These words are:

- ทรวด-ทรง (sûat-song - *shape, contour*)
- ทราม (saam - *low, inferior*)
- ทราบ (sâap - know *(formal)*)
- ทราย (saai - *sand*)

- ทรุด (sút - *sink*)
- อิน-ทรี (in-sii - *eagle*)
- มั่-ทรี (Mát-sii - *girl's name*)
- นน-ทรี (non-sii - *type of tree*)
- ทรวง (suang - *chest, breast*)
- ทรัพย์ (sáp - *wealth, property, estate*)
- ฉะ-เชิง-เทรา (Chà-chəəng-sao - *Thai province*)

- โทรม (soom - *shabby, worn out*)
- อิน-ทรีย์ (in-sii - *organic, organic fertiliser*)
- เทริด (sə̀ət - *crown*)
- พุ-ทรา (pút-saa - *type of fruit*)
- ไทร (sai - *Banyan Tree*)
- แทรก (sε̂εk - *insert*)

Appendix C.6 Classifiers for Nouns

One helpful aspect of learning Thai is that nouns are only ever singular and, unlike English, they do not need to be changed if or when they become plural. i.e. '*man*' does not become '*men*' in Thai, '*box*' does not become '*boxes*'.

This means you don't have to learn singular/plural forms but you need to learn the noun form classifiers to be able to correctly express quantities of nouns.

Appendix C.6.1 How Are Classifiers Used?

Where **no adjective** is present, the word order is normally:

noun + number + classifier

e.g. năng-sŭu-pim + sɔ̌ɔng + chà-bap = *newspaper + two + copies*

(หนัง-สือ-พิมพ์ + สอง + ฉ-บับ)

As a sentence this could be, "*Chăn ao năng-sŭu-pim sɔ̌ɔng chà-bap kâ.*" (ฉัน เอา หนัง-สือ-พิมพ์ สอง ฉ-บับ ค่ะ) = "*I want two newspapers.*"

Where there is an adjective present, the order within the phrase is most often

noun + adjective + number + classifier

e.g. biia + yài + nùng + kùat = *beer + large + one + bottle*

(เบียร์ + ใหญ่ + หนึ่ง + ขวด)

As a sentence: "*Pŏm ao biia yài nùng kùat kráp.*" (ผม เอา เบียร์ ใหญ่ หนึ่ง ขวด ครับ) = "*I would like a large bottle of beer please.*"

Note: In these examples we are illustrating how the sentence is structured and spoken in everyday Thai.

Appendix C.6.2 Common Classifiers

There are literally hundreds of classifiers in Thai language, here are some of the common ones:

- baan (บาน) for windows, doors, picture frames, mirrors, e.g. ประตู 2 บาน (*bprà-dtoo sɔ̌ɔng baan - 2 doors*)
- chà-bàp (ฉ-บับ) for letters, newspapers, e.g. จด-หมาย 3 ฉ-บับ (*jòt-mǎai saam chà-bàp - 3 letters*)
- gɛ̂ɛo (แก้ว) for drinking glasses, tumblers e.g. *Could I have a glass of beer please?* - pɔ̌m kɔ̌ɔ biia nɯ̀ng gɛ̂ɛo kráp (ผม ขอ เบียร์ หนึ่ง แก้ว ครับ)
- bai (ใบ) for empty glasses, e.g. *Could I have a glass please?* - chǎn kɔ̌ɔ gɛ̂ɛo nɯ̀ng bai kâ (ฉัน ขอ แก้ว หนึ่ง ใบ ค่ะ)
- dtôn (ต้น) for trees, plants, posts
- dtua (ตัว) for animals, insects, fish, tables and chairs, shirts, pants, coats, other living creatures
- duang (ดวง) for stars, postage stamps
- fɔɔng (ฟอง) for poultry eggs
- glàk (กลัก) for matchboxes
- gɔ̂ɔn (ก้อน) for lumps of sugar, stones
- hɔ̀ɔ (ห่อ) for bundles, parcels
- kon (คน) for a person, a child, human beings
- kûu (คู่) for pairs of articles, e.g. husband and wife, fork and spoon, etc.
- krɯ̂ɯang (เครื่อง) for electrical appliances: TVs, computers, phones, stereos, etc.
- lêem (เล่ม) for books, candles, scissors
- lam (ลำ) for boats, ships, aeroplanes
- mét (เม็ด) for smaller things, fruit pits, pills
- muan (มวน) for cigarettes
- pɛ̀ɛn (แผ่น) for sheets of paper, planks of wood
- ong (องค์) for holy personages, kings, and monks
- rɯɯan (เรือน) for clocks, watches
- rûup (รูป) for monks and novices, also for pictures
- sǎai (สาย) for roads, waterways, belts, etc
- sɔɔng (ซอง) for envelopes
- tûai (ถ้วย) for ceramic cups
- an (อัน) for small objects, things (in general)
- wong (วง) for rings, bracelets, a circle.

Appendix D. Writing Vowels and Other Characters

The following sections show you how to write all the Thai vowels and other language signs. Understanding the correct height of the vowels is important so we include two dashed lines to show the approximate base and height of the consonant.

Appendix D.1 Vowels

Remember, where possible, always start with the loop.

Vowels Before the Consonant

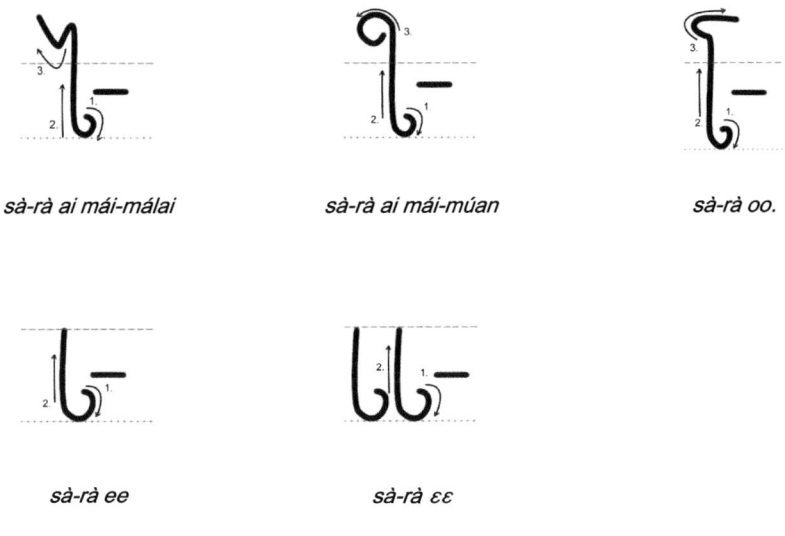

sà-rà ai mái-málai	*sà-rà ai mái-múan*	*sà-rà oo.*

sà-rà ee	*sà-rà εε*

Vowels After the Consonant

sà-rà am	*sà-rà a*	*sà-rà aa*

Vowels Below the Consonant

sà-rà u   sà-rà uu

Vowels Above the Consonant

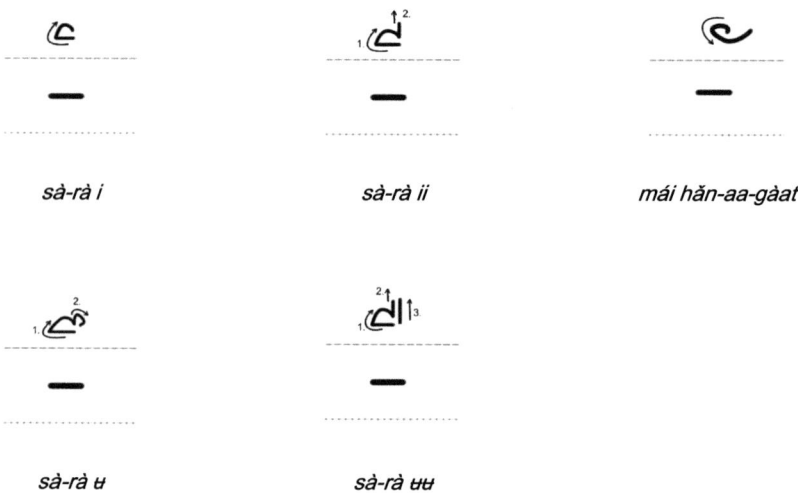

sà-rà i   sà-rà ii   mái hăn-aa-gàat

sà-rà ʉ   sà-rà ʉʉ

Remember, vowels are always written in the same place and if you are writing a complex vowel such as the tripthong sà-rà /ʉʉa/ (เ-ือ) then this is comprised of three individual vowels as shown:

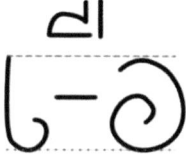

Appendix D.2 Signs

Here we have the tone marks and other signs used in written Thai:

Tone Marks

mái èek

mái too

mái dtrii

mái jàt-dtà-waa

Other Signs

Writing Mái Yá-mók, Bpee-yaan-nɔ́ɔi, Bpee-yaan-yài, Gaa-ran and Mái-dtài-kúu:

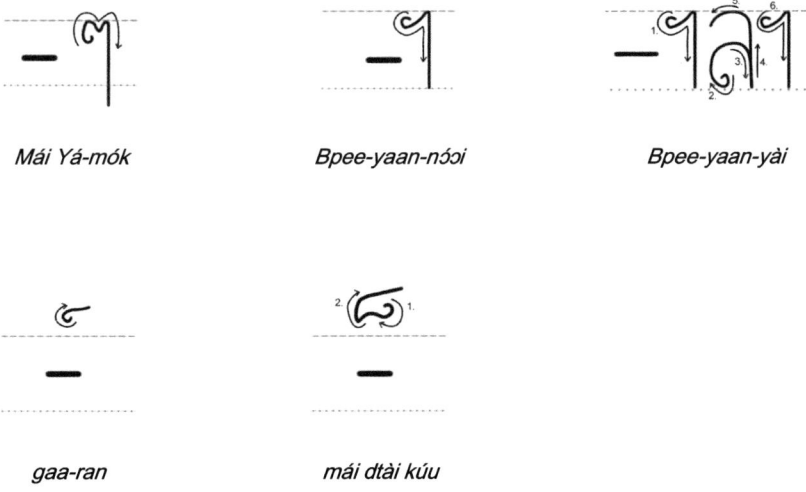

Mái Yá-mók

Bpee-yaan-nɔ́ɔi

Bpee-yaan-yài

gaa-ran

mái dtài kúu

Appendix E. Numbers, Counting and Time

This section explains numbers, counting in Thai and how to tell the time.

Before we can discuss the time we need to be familiar with numbers.

Appendix E.1 Numbers

Below is the full list of numbers 1 to 99 and then the important numbers above that, 100, 1,000, 10,000, etc.

You will see that *one* is pronounced nɯ̀ng, yet 11, 21, and so on, use the suffix -èt (-เอ็ด)

Appendix E.2 Counting

The difference between counting in English and counting in Thai is that you have to be specific about each group of numbers.

For example, with the number 2,367,458, we would say, "Two million, three hundred and sixty-seven thousand, four hundred and fifty-eight."

However, in Thai, you would say, "Two million, three hundred thousand, sixty thousand, seven thousand, four hundred, fifty-eight."

Or actually in [transliterated] Thai:

"sɔ̌ɔng-láan sǎam-sɛ̌ɛn hòk-mɯ̀ɯn jèt-pan sìi-rói hâa-sìp-bpɛ̀ɛt (สอง-ล้าน สาม-แสน หก-หมื่น เจ็ด-พัน สี่-ร้อย ห้า-สิบ-แปด).

This is, of course, ๒,๓๖๗,๔๕๘ in Thai numerals.

0 - ๐ - sǔun (ศูนย์)	13 - sìp-sǎam (สิบ-สาม)
1 - ๑ - nɯ̀ng (หนึ่ง)	14 - sìp-sìi (สิบ-สี่)
2 - ๒ - sɔ̌ɔng (สอง)	15 - sìp-hâa (สิบ-ห้า)
3 - ๓ - sǎam (สาม)	16 - sìp-hòk (สิบ-หก)
4 - ๔ - sìi (สี่)	17 - sìp-jèt (สิบ-เจ็ด)
5 - ๕ - hâa (ห้า)	18 - sìp-bpɛ̀ɛt (สิบ-แปด)
6 - ๖ - hòk (หก)	19 - sìp-gâo (สิบ-เก้า)
7 - ๗ - jèt (เจ็ด)	20 - yîi-sìp (ยี่-สิบ)
8 - ๘ - bpɛ̀ɛt (แปด)	21- yîi-sìp-èt (ยี่-สิบ-เอ็ด)
9 - ๙ - gâo (เก้า)	22- yîi-sìp-sɔ̌ɔng (ยี่-สิบ-สอง)
10 - ๑๐ - sìp (สิบ)	23 - yîi-sìp-sǎam (ยี่-สิบ-สาม)
11 - sìp-èt (สิบ-เอ็ด)	24 - yîi-sìp-sìi (ยี่-สิบ-สี่)
12 - sìp-sɔ̌ɔng (สิบ-สอง)	25 - yîi-sìp-hâa (ยี่-สิบ-ห้า)

26 - yîi-sìp-hòk (ยี่-สิบ-หก)

27 - yîi-sìp-jèt (ยี่-สิบ-เจ็ด)

28 - yîi-sìp-bpɛ̀ɛt (ยี่-สิบ-แปด)

29 - yîi-sìp-gâo (ยี่-สิบ-เก้า)

30 - sǎam-sìp (สาม-สิบ)

31 - sǎam-sìp-èt (สาม-สิบ-เอ็ด)

32 - sǎam-sìp-sɔ̌ɔng (สาม-สิบ-สอง)

33 - sǎam-sìp-sǎam (สาม-สิบ-สาม)

34 - sǎam-sìp-sìi (สาม-สิบ-สี่)

35 - sǎam-sìp-hâa (สาม-สิบ-ห้า)

36 - sǎam-sìp-hòk (สาม-สิบ-หก)

37 - sǎam-sìp-jèt (สาม-สิบ-เจ็ด)

38 - sǎam-sìp-bpɛ̀ɛt (สาม-สิบ-แปด)

39 - sǎam-sìp-gâo (สาม-สิบ-เก้า)

40 - sìi-sìp (สี่-สิบ)

41 - sìi-sìp-èt (สี่-สิบ-เอ็ด)

42 - sìi-sìp-sɔ̌ɔng (สี่-สิบ-สอง)

43 - sìi-sìp-sǎam (สี่-สิบ-สาม)

44 - sìi-sìp-sìi (สี่-สิบ-สี่)

45 - sìi-sìp-hâa (สี่-สิบ-ห้า)

46 - sìi-sìp-hòk (สี่-สิบ-หก)

47 - sìi-sìp-jèt (สี่-สิบ-เจ็ด)

48 - sìi-sìp-bpɛ̀ɛt (สี่-สิบ-แปด)

49 - sìi-sìp-gâo (สี่-สิบ-เก้า)

50 - hâa-sìp (ห้า-สิบ)

51 - hâa-sìp-èt (ห้า-สิบ-เอ็ด)

52 - hâa-sìp-sɔ̌ɔng (ห้า-สิบ-สอง)

53 - hâa-sìp-sǎam (ห้า-สิบ-สาม)

54 - hâa-sìp-sìi (ห้า-สิบ-สี่)

55 - hâa-sìp-hâa (ห้า-สิบ-ห้า)

56 - hâa-sìp-hòk (ห้า-สิบ-หก)

57 - hâa-sìp-jèt (ห้า-สิบ-เจ็ด)

58 - hâa-sìp-bpɛ̀ɛt (ห้า-สิบ-แปด)

59 - hâa-sìp-gâo (ห้า-สิบ-เก้า)

60 - hòk-sìp (หก-สิบ)

61 - hòk-sìp-èt (หก-สิบ-เอ็ด)

62 - hòk-sìp-sɔ̌ɔng (หก-สิบ-สอง)

63 - hòk-sìp-sǎam (หก-สิบ-สาม)

64 - hòk-sìp-sìi (หก-สิบ-สี่)

65 - hòk-sìp-hâa (หก-สิบ-ห้า)

66 - hòk-sìp-hòk (หก-สิบ-หก)

67 - hòk-sìp-jèt (หก-สิบ-เจ็ด)

68 - hòk-sìp-bpɛ̀ɛt (หก-สิบ-แปด)

69 - hòk-sìp-gâo (หก-สิบ-เก้า)

70 - jèt-sìp (เจ็ด-สิบ)

71 - jèt-sìp-èt (เจ็ด-สิบ-เอ็ด)

72 - jèt-sìp-sɔ̌ɔng (เจ็ด-สิบ-สอง)

73 - jèt-sìp-sǎam (เจ็ด-สิบ-สาม)

74 - jèt-sìp-sìi (เจ็ด-สิบ-สี่)

75 - jèt-sìp-hâa (เจ็ด-สิบ-ห้า)

76 - jèt-sìp-hòk (เจ็ด-สิบ-หก)

77 - jèt-sìp-jèt (เจ็ด-สิบ-เจ็ด)

78 - jèt-sìp-bpɛ̀ɛt (เจ็ด-สิบ-แปด)

79 - jèt-sìp-gâo (เจ็ด-สิบ-เก้า)

80 - bpɛ̀ɛt -sìp (แปด-สิบ)

81 - bpɛ̀ɛt-sìp-èt (แปด-สิบ-เอ็ด)

82 - bpɛ̀ɛt-sìp-sɔ̌ɔng (แปด-สิบ-สอง)

83 - bpὲɛt-sìp-sǎam (แปด-สิบ-สาม)

84 - bpὲɛt-sìp-sìi (แปด-สิบ-สี่)

85 - bpὲɛt-sìp-hâa (แปด-สิบ-ห้า)

86 - bpὲɛt-sìp-hòk (แปด-สิบ-หก)

87 - bpὲɛt-sìp-jèt (แปด-สิบ-เจ็ด)

88 - bpὲɛt-sìp-bpὲɛt (แปด-สิบ-แปด)

89 - bpὲɛt-sìp-gâo (แปด-สิบ-เก้า)

90 - gâo-sìp (เก้า-สิบ)

91 - gâo-sìp-èt (เก้า-สิบ-เอ็ด)

92 - gâo-sìp-sɔ̌ɔng (เก้า-สิบ-สอง)

93 - gâo-sìp-sǎam (เก้า-สิบ-สาม)

94 - gâo-sìp-sìi (เก้า-สิบ-สี่)

95 - gâo-sìp-hâa (เก้า-สิบ-ห้า)

96 - gâo-sìp-hòk (เก้า-สิบ-หก)

97 - gâo-sìp-jèt (เก้า-สิบ-เจ็ด)

98 - gâo-sìp-bpὲɛt (เก้า-สิบ-แปด)

99 - gâo-sìp-gâo (เก้า-สิบ-เก้า)

100 - nὲng rɔ́ɔi (หนึ่ง ร้อย)

101 - nὲng rɔ́ɔi èt (หนึ่ง ร้อย เอ็ด)

111 - nὲng rɔ́ɔi sìp-èt (หนึ่ง ร้อย-สิบ-เอ็ด)

300 - sǎam-rɔ́ɔi (สาม-ร้อย)

900 - gâo-rɔ́ɔi (เก้า-ร้อย)

1000 - nὲng pan (หนึ่ง พัน)

10,000 - nὲng mὲɯn (หนึ่ง หมื่น)

100,000 - nὲng sɛ̌ɛn (หนึ่ง แสน)

1,000,000 - nὲng láan (หนึ่ง ล้าน)

Appendix E.3 Time

Two methods of time are used in Thailand: the first is the 24-hour clock. This is used to some extent in bus stations, train stations, government buildings, airports, etc., but elsewhere a totally different system is used.

This second system is where the day is broken down into 4 periods of 5 or 6 hours each. The difficulty with this method is that each period is referred to differently.

0100 to 0500 - the hour is preceeded by dtii (ตี):

Informal (Speaking)	Formal
• 1 am - dtii nὲng (ตี หนึ่ง)	• nὲng naa-lí-gaa (หนึ่ง นา-ฬิ-กา)
• 2 am - dtii sɔ̌ɔng (ตี สอง)	• sɔ̌ɔng naa-lí-gaa (สอง นา-ฬิ-กา)
• 3 am - dtii sǎam (ตี สาม)	• sǎam naa-lí-gaa (สาม นา-ฬิ-กา)
• 4 am - dtii sìi (ตี สี่)	• sìi naa-lí-gaa (สี่ นา-ฬิ-กา)
• 5 am - dtii hâa (ตี ห้า)	• hâa naa-lí-gaa (ห้า นา-ฬิ-กา)

• Dtrong (ตรง) means *straight* and refers to the exact hour.

0600 to 1100 - the hour is followed by moong cháo (โมง เช้า):

Informal (Speaking)	Formal
• 6 am - hòk moong cháo (หก โมง เช้า)	hòk naa-lí-gaa (หก นา-ฬิ-กา)
• 7 am - jèt moong cháo (เจ็ด โมง เช้า)	jèt naa-lí-gaa (เจ็ด นา-ฬิ-กา)
• 8 am - bpɛ̀ɛt moong cháo (แปด โมง เช้า)	bpɛ̀ɛt naa-lí-gaa (แปด นา-ฬิ-กา)
• 9 am - gâo moong cháo (เก้า โมง เช้า)	gâo naa-lí-gaa (เก้า นา-ฬิ-กา)
• 10 am - sìp moong cháo (สิบ โมง เช้า)	sìp naa-lí-gaa (สิบ นา-ฬิ-กา)
• 11 am - sìp-èt moong cháo (สิบ-เอ็ด โมง เช้า)	sìp-èt naa-lí-gaa (สิบ-เอ็ด นา-ฬิ-กา)
• Midday - tîiang dtrong (เที่ยง ตรง)	sìp-sɔ̌ɔng naa-lí-gaa (สิบ-สอง นา-ฬิ-กา)

1300 to 1500 - the hour is preceeded by bàai (บ่าย), meaning early afternoon:

Informal (Speaking)	Formal
• 1 pm - bàai (nὺng) moong (บ่าย (หนึ่ง) โมง)	sìp-sǎam naa-lí-gaa (สิบ-สาม นา-ฬิ-กา)
• 2 pm - bàai sɔ̌ɔng (moong) (บ่าย สอง (โมง))	sìp-sìi naa-lí-gaa (สิบ-สี่ นา-ฬิ-กา)
• 3 pm - bàai sǎam (moong) (บ่าย สาม (โมง))	sìp-hâa naa-lí-gaa (สิบ-ห้า นา-ฬิ-กา)

1600 to 1800 - the hour is followed by yen (เย็น), meaning late afternoon:

Informal (Speaking)	Formal
• 4 pm - sìi moong yen (สี่ โมง เย็น)	sìp-hòk naa-lí-gaa (สิบ-หก นา-ฬิ-กา)
• 5 pm - hâa moong yen (ห้า โมง เย็น)	sìp-jèt naa-lí-gaa (สิบ-เจ็ด นา-ฬิ-กา)
• 6 pm - hòk moong yen (หก โมง เย็น)	sìp-bpɛ̀ɛt naa-lí-gaa (สิบ-แปด นา-ฬิ-กา)

1900 to 2300 - the hour is followed by tûm (ทุ่ม):

Informal (Speaking)	Formal
• 7 pm - nèng tûm (หนึ่ง ทุ่ม)	sìp-gâo naa-lí-gaa (สิบ-เก้า นา-ฬิ-กา)
• 8 pm - sɔ̌ɔng tûm (สอง ทุ่ม)	yîi-sìp naa-lí-gaa (ยี่-สิบ นา-ฬิ-กา)
• 9 pm - sǎam tûm (สาม ทุ่ม)	yîi-sìp-èt naa-lí-gaa (ยี่-สิบ-เอ็ด นา-ฬิ-กา)
• 10 pm - sìi tûm (สี่ ทุ่ม)	yîi-sìp-sɔ̌ɔng naa-lí-gaa (ยี่-สิบ-สอง นา-ฬิ-กา)
• 11 pm - hâa tûm (ห้า ทุ่ม)	yîi-sìp-sǎam naa-lí-gaa (ยี่-สิบ-สาม นา-ฬิ-กา)
• Midnight - tîiang kʉʉn (เที่ยง คืน)	yîi-sìp-sìi naa-lí-gaa (ยี่-สิบ-สี่ นา-ฬิ-กา)

Note: You may hear midnight being referred to as hòk tûm (หก ทุ่ม), but it is rarely used.

Appendix E.3.1 Confusion?

Early Mornings

There can occasionally be some confusion when referring to time in the second period of the day, 0600 - 1100 (or more precisely, from 0700). Though this method of telling the time is not used as much nowadays, it can still be referred to.

Time can be referred to in two ways: as we have written above, i.e. hòk moong cháo (หก โมง เช้า), 7 am - jèt moong cháo (เจ็ด โมง เช้า), etc. or it can be referred to as the, '1st hour of the morning', the '2nd hour of the morning', etc.

6 am - *hòk moong cháo* (หก โมง เช้า) - sixth hour morning

7 am - *nèng moong cháo* (หนึ่ง โมง เช้า) - 1st hour morning

8 am - *sɔ̌ɔng moong cháo* (สอง โมง เช้า) - 2nd hour morning

9 am - *sǎam moong cháo* (สาม โมง เช้า) - 3rdhour morning

10 am - *sìi moong cháo* (สี่ โมง เช้า) - 4th hour morning

11 am - *hâa moong cháo* (ห้า โมง เช้า) - 5th hour morning

Here you can see where confusion could arise: 6 am, which is always referred to as *hòk moong cháo* (หก โมง เช้า), is the *6th hour of the morning* yet 7 am, which comes after 6 am, is referred to as the *1st hour of the morning*.

Personally, I prefer to refer to the 7th and subsequent hours as เจ็ด โมง เช้า, แปด โมง เช้า, etc., as it avoids any confusion.

Good Afternoon

Some also say that 4pm in our afternoon transition period should be classed as *bàai sii moong* (บ่าย สี่ โมง) and not as written, *sii moong yen* (สี่ โมง เย็น): it all depends on your definition of 'late afternoon'.

Appendix F. Useful Phrases

Here are some more useful, basic conversational phrases to help you in the Land of Smiles. Don't forget to use kâ or kráp (as appropriate) and always remember, a smile goes a long way, everywhere!

Appendix F.1 Basic Conversation

- Yes - *châi* (ใช่) or *kráp* (ครับ) or *kâ* (ค่ะ): *kráp/kâ* can also be used to indicate agreement.
- No - *mâi* (ไม่) or *mâi châi* (ไม่ ใช่)
- Thank you - *kɔ̀ɔp-kun* (ขอบ-คุณ)
- Hello - *sà-wàt-dii* (ส-วัส-ดี)
- How are you/are you well? - *kun sà-baai dii mǎi* (คุณ ส-บาย ดี ไหม)
- I'm fine/I'm well - *pǒm sà-baai dii* (ผม ส-บาย ดี)
- Not well - *mâi sà-baai* (ไม่ ส-บาย)
- Good luck - *chôok dii* (โชค ดี)
- Please - *gà-rú-naa* (ก-รุ-ณา)

Appendix F.2 About Yourself

- My name is... (male) - *pǒm chɯ̂ɯ...* (ผม ชื่อ...)
- My name is .... (female) - *dì-chǎn chɯ̂ɯ...* (ดิ-ฉัน ชื่อ ...)
- What's your name? - *kun chɯ̂ɯ à-rai* (คุณ ชื่อ อะ-ไร)
- His/her name is... - *kǎo chɯ̂ɯ..* (เขา ชื่อ...)
- How old are you? - *kun aa-yú tâo rài* (คุณ อา-ยุ เท่า ไหร่)
- I am 30 years old - *pǒm aa-yú sǎam-sip bpii* (ผม อา-ยุ สาม-สิบ ปี)

Appendix F.3 Asking Questions

- Where? - *tîi-nǎi* (ที่-ไหน), e.g. Where is the toilet? - *hɔ̂ɔng nám yùu tîi-nǎi* (ห้อง นำ อยู่ ที่-ไหน)
- Who? - *krai* (ใคร), e.g. Who is that? - *nân kɯɯ krai* (นั่น คือ ใคร)
- Whose? - *kɔ̌ɔng krai* (ของ ใคร), e.g. Whose pen is that? - *nân kɯɯ bpàak-gaa kɔ̌ɔng krai* (นั่น คือ ปาก-กา ของ ใคร)
- Why? - *tam-mai* (ทำ-ไม), e.g. Why did you say that? - *tam-mai kun pûut bὲɛp nán* (ทำ-ไม คุณ พูด แบบ นั่น)

- What? - *à-rai* (อะ-ไร), e.g. What is the time? - *wee-laa à-rai lέεο* (เว-ลา อะ-ไร แล้ว) or you can use *gii moong lέεο* (กี่ โมง แล้ว)
- When? - *mûua-rài* (เมื่อ-ไหร่), e.g. When does the shop open? - *ráan bpòət mûua-rài* (ร้าน เปิด เมื่อ-ไหร่)
- Please speak slowly - *gà-rú-naa pûut cháa cháa nòoi* (ก-รุ-ณา พูด ช้าๆ หน่อย)
- Can you speak English? - *kun pûut paa-săa ang-grit dâi măi* (คุณ พูด ภา-ษา อัง-กฤษ ได้ ไหม)
- What's that? - *nân kuu à-rai* (นั่น คือ อะไร)
- Please repeat that - *gà-rú-naa pûut iik tii* (ก-รุ-ณา พูด อีก ที)

Appendix F.4 Other Useful Expressions and Phrases

- Excuse me - *kɔ̌ɔ-tôot* (ขอ-โทษ)
- Sorry (apology) - *kɔ̌ɔ-tôot* (ขอ-โทษ)
- Sorry (feeling regret) - *sĭa jai* (เสีย ใจ)
- I don't speak Thai - *pŏm pûut tai mâi dâi* (ผม พูด ไทย ไม่ ได้)
- I already have one - *chăn mii lέεο* (ฉัน มี แล้ว)
- I don't have one - *pŏm mâi mii* (ผม ไม่ มี)
- I don't have one now - *chăn mâi mii lέεο* (ฉัน ไม่ มี แล้ว)
- I'm sorry, I don't understand - *kɔ̌ɔ-tôot kráp pŏm mâi kâo-jai* (ขอ-โทษ ครับ ผม ไม่ เข้า-ใจ)
- No, thank you, I don't want it - *chăn mâi ao kâ kɔ̌ɔp-kun kâ* (ฉัน ไม่ เอา ค่ะ ขอบ-คุณ ค่ะ)

Appendix G. Lists

The next few pages details lists of items that will help expand your vocabulary and include such items as *Personal Pronouns*, *Verbs*, *Nouns*, *Adjectives*, *Cooking Terms*, etc.

Appendix G.1 Personal Pronouns

The following is the list of most common personal pronouns. There are more but just learning these will see you well on your way to conversing effectively in Thai.

- *I, me* - pŏm (ผม) (formal) is a polite word used only by males.
- *I, me* - dì-chăn (ดิ-ฉัน) (formal) is a polite word used only by females.
- *I, me* - chăn (ฉัน) (informal)

  This is another personal pronoun that is used by both men and women; it is not something that you hear in day-to-day use. It is a word that is used amongst intimates, with very close friends, or when you are talking to people of a lower social rank than you, i.e. servants.

Never use it with people of a higher rank or social status than yourself.

- *You* - təə (เธอ)

  This is another very familiar form of address. It is used mainly by women talking to each other. It is often used in conjunction with chăn (above).

- *You* - kun (คุณ) is a polite word used by males and females. This is the word most commonly heard in daily conversation.
- *He, she* - kăo (เขา) is used by either sex referring to just about anyone.
- *You, he, she* - tâan (ท่าน) is used when talking to a person of higher rank than yourself, e.g. to monks, to the Prime Minister, etc.
- *They* - pûak-kăo (พวก-เขา)
- *We, us* - pûak-rao (พวก-เรา)

Appendix G.2 Verbs

- *Ask* - tâam (ถาม)
- *Bite* - gàt (กัด)
- *Brush* - bprɛɛng (แปรง)
- *Climb* - bpiin (ปีน)
- *Come* - maa (มา)
- *Cook* - tam aa-hăan (ทำ อา-หาร)
- *Cry* - rɔ́ɔng-hâi (ร้อง-ไห้)
- *Cut* - dtàt (ตัด)
- *Dance* - dtêen-ram (เต้น-รำ)
- *Do* - tam (ทำ)
- *Drink* - dɯ̀ɯm (ดื่ม)
- *Drive* - kàp (ขับ)
- *Eat* - gin (กิน)
- *Find* - jəə (เจอ)
- *Forget* - lɯɯm (ลืม)
- *Go* - bpai (ไป)
- *Have* - mii (มี)
- *Hear* - dâi-yin (ได้-ยิน)
- *Help* - chûai (ช่วย)
- *Jump* - grà-dòot (กระ-โดด)
- *Know (something)* - rúu (รู้)
- *Know (someone)* - rúu-jàk (รู้-จัก)

- *Learn* - riian-rúu (เรียน-รู้)
- *Like* - chɔ̂ɔp (ชอบ)
- *Listen* - fang (ฟัง)
- *Look* - duu (ดู)
- *Look for* - mɔɔng-hăa (มอง-หา)
- *Love* - rák (รัก)
- *Meet* - póp (พบ)
- *Need* - jam-bpen-dtɔ̂ɔng (จำ-เป็น-ต้อง)
- *Play* - lêen (เล่น)
- *Pull* - dɯng (ดึง)
- *Push* - plàk (ผลัก)
- *Put (down)* - waang (วาง)
- *Read* - àan (อ่าน)
- *Remember* - jam (จำ)
- *Ride* - kii (ขี่)
- *Run* - wîng (วิ่ง)
- *See* - hĕn (เห็น)
- *Sing* - rɔ́ɔng-pleeng (ร้อง-เพลง)
- *Sit* - nâng (นั่ง)
- *Sleep* - nɔɔn (นอน)
- *Stand* - yɯɯn (ยืน)

- *Study* - riian (เรียน)
- *Swim* - wâai (ว่าย)
- *Teach* - sɔ̌ɔn (สอน)
- *Think* - kít (คิด)
- *Understand* - kâo-jai (เข้า-ใจ)
- *Use* - chái (ใช้)
- *Walk* - dəən (เดิน)
- *Want* - dtɔ̂ɔng-gaan (ต้อง-การ)
- *Watch* - fâo-duu (เฝ้า-ดู)
- *Write* - kǐian (เขียน).

Appendix G.3 Adjectives

- *Big* - yài (ใหญ่)
- *Little* - nít-nɔ̀ɔi (นิด-หน่อย)
- *Fast* - réo (เร็ว)
- *Slow* - cháa (ช้า)
- *Happy* - mii kwaam sùk (มี ความ สุข)
- *Sad* - sâo (เศร้า)
- *Long* - yaao (ยาว)
- *Short* - dtîia (เตี้ย)
- *Loud* - dang (ดัง)
- *Quiet* - ngîiap (เงียบ)
- *Tall* - sǔung (สูง)
- *Small* - lék (เล็ก)
- *Angry* - gròot (โกรธ)
- *Difficult, hard* - yâak (ยาก)
- *Warm (friendly)* - òp-ùn (อบ-อุ่น)
- *Friendly* - bpen-mít (เป็น-มิตร)
- *Hostile* - mâi bpen-mít (ไม่ เป็น-มิตร)
- *Hard, heavy* - nàk (หนัก)
- *Easy* - ngâai (ง่าย)
- *Light (weight)* - bao (เบา)
- *Dark* - mûut (มืด)
- *Light (bright)* - sà-wàang (สว่าง)
- *Good* - dii (ดี)
- *Bad* - leeo (เลว)

- *Beautiful* - sǔai (สวย)
- *Ugly* - nâa-glìat (น่า-เกลียด)
- *Hungry* - hǐo (หิว)
- *Full (up - with food)* - ìm (อิ่ม)
- *Strong* - kěng-rɛɛng (แข็ง-แรง)
- *Weak* - ɔ̀ɔn-ɛɛ (อ่อน-แอ)
- *Old* - gào (เก่า)
- *Young (adolescent)* - nùm (male), sǎao (female) (หนุ่ม, สาว)
- *Rich* - ruai (รวย)
- *Poor* - jon (จน)
- *Expensive* - pɛɛng (แพง)
- *Cheap* - tùuk (ถูก).

Appendix G.4 Seasons

Thailand has three seasons (season is called rʉ́-duu (ฤ-ดู)), hot, rainy and cold. These are:

- *Hot season* (March to May) - *rʉ́-duu rɔ́ɔn* (ฤ-ดู ร้อน)
- *Rainy season* (June to October) - *rʉ́-duu fǒn* (ฤ-ดู ฝน)
- *Cold season* (November to February) - *rʉ́-duu nǎao* (ฤ-ดู หนาว).

Appendix G.5 Colours
- *Black* - sǐi dam (สี ดำ)
- *Blue* - sǐi fáa (สี ฟ้า)
- *Brown* - sǐi nám-dtaan (สี น้ำ-ตาล)
- *Gold* - sǐi tɔɔng (สี ทอง)
- *Gray* - sǐi tao (สี เทา)
- *Green* - sǐi kǐiao (สี เขียว)
- *Khaki* - sǐi gaa-gìi (สี กา-กี)
- *Orange* - sǐi sôm (สี ส้ม)
- *Purple* - sǐi mûang (สี ม่วง)
- *Pink* - sǐi chom-puu (สี ชม-พู)
- *Red* - sǐi dɛɛng (สี แดง)

- *Silver* - sĭi ngəən (สี เงิน)
- *White* - sĭi khăao (สี ขาว).

Appendix G.6 Food /Cooking Terms

Thai people love food and talking or thinking about food is almost like the English fixation with the weather, it's almost a lifestyle.

The following is just a small sample of the many wonderful dishes and flavours that can be gotten almost anywhere - delicious!

Cooking Terms

- *Boil* - dtôm (ต้ม)
- *Steam* - nûng (นึ่ง) (you may also hear it being called dtŭn (ตุ๋น))
- *Deep fried* - tɔ̂ɔd (ทอด)
- *Toast* - bpîng (ปิ้ง)
- *Bake* - òp (อบ)
- *Barbeque, grill, roast* - yâang (ย่าง)
- *Fry* - pàt (ผัด).

Commenting

- *Delicious* - à-rɔ̀ɔi (อ-ร่อย)
- *Not delicious* - mâi à-rɔ̀ɔi (ไม่ อ-ร่อย)
- *Very delicious* - à-rɔ̀ɔi mâak (อ-ร่อย มาก)
- *Spicy* - pèt (เผ็ด)
- *Not spicy* - mâi pèt (ไม่ เผ็ด)
- *Very Spicy* - pèt mâak (เผ็ด มาก)
- *Sweet* - wăan (หวาน)
- *Sour* - bprîiao (เปรี้ยว)
- *Salty* - kem (เค็ม)
- *Bitter* - kŏm (ขม).

Food

- *Rice* - kâao (ข้าว) or you may see ข้าว สวย (kâao sŭai - *cooked rice*)

- *Sticky rice* - kâao nĭiao (ข้าว เหนียว)
- *Chicken* - gài (ไก่)
- *Pork* - mŭu (หมู)
- *Beef* - núɐa (เนื้อ)
- *Fish* - bplaa (ปลา)
- *Chilli* - prík (พริก)
- *Mushroom* - hèt (เห็ด)
- *Onion* - hɔ̆ɔm-hŭa-yài (หอม-หัว-ใหญ่).

Dishes

A selection of some of my favourite Thai dishes:

- *Chicken with chillies* - gài pàt prík yùak (ไก่ ผัด พริก หยวก)
- *Chicken with basil and chillies* - gà-prao gài (กะ-เพรา ไก่)
- *Noodles* - gŭai dtĭiao (ก๋วย เตี๋ยว)
- *Green sweet chicken curry* - gɛɛng kĭiao wăan gài (แกง เขียว หวาน ไก่)
- *Thai vermicelli* - kà-nŏm jiin (ข-นม จีน)
- *Rice soup* - kâao dtôm (ข้าว ต้ม)
- *Spicy soup with shrimp* - dtôm yam gûng (ต้ม ยำ กุ้ง)
- *Spicy soup with chicken* - dtôm yam gài (ต้ม ยำ ไก่)
- *Noodles Thai style* - pàd Thai (ผัด ไทย)
- *Omelette* - kài jiiao (ไข่ เจียว)
- *Papaya salad* - sôm-dtam (ส้ม-ตำ)
- *Minced pork salad* - lâap (ลาบ).

Appendix G.7 Drinks
- *Water* - nám (น้ำ)
- *Orange* - sôm (ส้ม)

- *Orange juice* - nám sôm (น้ำ ส้ม)
- *Grapefruit* - sôm-oo (ส้ม-โอ)
- *Grapefruit juice* - nám sôm-oo (น้ำ ส้ม-โอ)
- *Pineapple* - sàp-bpà-rót (สับ-ปะ-รด)
- *Coffee* - gaa-fɛɛ (กา-แฟ)
- *Tea* – chaa (ชา)
- *Coke* - kóok (โค้ก)
- *Ice* - náam kěng (น้ำ แข็ง)
- *Beer* - biia (เบียร์)
- *Wine* - wai (ไวน์).

Appendix G.8 Occupations

- *"Kun tam-ngaan à-rai kráp"* (คุณ ทำ-งาน อะ-ไร ครับ) - *"You work what?/What work do you do?"*
- *Cook* (male) - *pɔ̂ɔ-krua* (พ่อ-ครัว)
- *Cook* (female) - *mɛ̂ɛ-krua* (แม่-ครัว)
- *Dentist* - mɔ̌ɔ-fan (หมอ-ฟัน)
- *Doctor* - mɔ̌ɔ (หมอ), pɛ̂ɛt (แพทย์)
- *Electrician* - châang-fai-fáa (ช่าง-ไฟ-ฟ้า)
- *Engineer* - wít-sà-wá-gɔɔn (วิ-ศ-ว-กร)

- *Farmer* - chaao-naa (ชาว-นา)
- *Hairdresser* - châang-tam-pŏm (ช่าง-ทำ-ผม)
- *Lawyer* - tá-naai-kwaam (ท-นาย-ความ)
- *Mechanic* - châang-gon (ช่าง-กล)
- *Nurse* - pá-yaa-baan (พ-ยา-บาล)
- *Pilot* - nák-bin (นัก-บิน)
- *Policeman* - dtam-rùat (ตำ-รวจ)
- *Postman* - bù-rùt-bprai-sà-nii (บุ-รุษ-ไปร-ษ-ณีย์)
- *Sailor* - gà-laa-sǐi ɾʉʉa (กะ-ลา-สี เรือ)
- *Secretary* - lee-kǎa-nú-gaan (เล-ขา-นุ-การ)
- *Teacher* - kruu, aa-jaan (ครู, อา-จารย์)
- *Businessman* - nák-tú-rá-git (นัก-ธุ-ร-กิจ)
- *Business owner* - jâo-kǒong tú-rá-git (เจ้า-ของ ธุ-ร-กิจ)
- *Manager* - pûu-jàt-gaan (ผู้-จัด-การ)
- *Student* - nák-riian (นัก-เรียน).

Nudibranch - Boonsung wreck

Appendix H. Bibliography

- Robson S. & Changchit P., 2007. *Instant Thai.* Tuttle Publishing, 2007

- Becker BP., 1995. *Thai for Beginners.* Paiboon Publishing, 1995

- Becker BP., 1998. *Thai for Intermediate Learners.* Paiboon Publishing, 1998

- Becker BP. & Pirazzi C., 2009. *Three-way Thai-English Dictionary.* Paiboon Publishing, 2009.

- Jai-Ua B., & Golding M., 2003. *Pocket Thai Dictionary.* Periplus, 2003

- กำชัย ทองหล่อ, 2552. หลักภาษาไทย. อมรการพิมพ์ กทม, 2552

- *Thai2English* - Nectec - http://www.thaienglish.com

- Campbell S., & Shaweevong C., 2006. (Online) *The Fundamentals of the Thai Language.* Available at: http://www.lyndonhill.com (Accessed: 05/04/2010)

- Muay Thai Fighting, 17/02/2008. *Muay Thai Rules* (Online) Available at http://www.muaythai-fighting.com (Accessed: 10/11/2010)

- Wikepedia.*Culture of Thailand* (Online) Available at http://en.wikipedia.org/wiki/Culture_of_Thailand (Accessed: 17/10/2010)

- Siam Foundation. *What are the Buddhist Precepts?* (Online) Available at http://siamfoundation.org/thailand-faq/index.php?action=artikel&cat=5&id=3&artlang=en (Accessed: 22/10/2010)

- http://www.paknam.com (Accessed online: 9th October 2010)

- http://www.thai-language.com/ (Accessed online: 9th October 2010)

- http://www.siamfoundation.org (Accessed online: 9th October 2010)

- http://www.learningthai.com (Accessed online: 17th August 2010)

- http://www.slice-of-thai.com/ (Accessed online: 17th August 2010)

- http://www.rusiedotton.thai.net (Accessed online: 23rd November 2010)

Index

A

A lot - mâak (มาก) 17

Aa (อา) - father's younger brother or sister 62

Aa-gàat (อากาศ) - weather, climate 96

Aa-hăan (อาหาร)

    Aa-hăan (อาหาร) - food 35, 54

    Aa-hăan cháo (อาหารเช้า) - breakfast 36

    Aa-hăan jiin (อาหารจีน) - Chinese food 68

    Aa-hăan prɔ́ɔm lɛ́ɛo (อาหารพร้อมแล้ว) - food is ready 56

    Aa-hăan tai (อาหารไทย) - Thai food 68

    Aa-hăan tîiang (อาหารเที่ยง) - lunch 36, 54

    Aa-hăan yen (อาหารเย็น) - dinner 36, 106

Àan (อ่าน) - read 52, 155

Àang (อ่าง) - bowl 131

Aa-tít (อาทิตย์) - week 74

Àat-jà (อาจจะ) - maybe, might 52, 53, 72

Abate - lót-long (ลดลง) 131

Abbreviation sign - ๆ (bpee-yaan-nɔ́ɔi เปยาลน้อย) 140

Able

    able, can - dâi (ได้) 85

    able, can - săa-mâat (สามารถ) 72

Add, put in - sài (ใส่) 125

Adult - pûu-yài (ผู้ใหญ่) 60

After tomorrow - má-ruun-nii (มะรืนนี้) 74

Afternoon late, dusk, evening - dtɔɔn yen (ตอนเย็น) 36

Again

    Again - iik (อีก) 31, 35, 131

    Again - mài (ใหม่) 141

Age - aa-yú (อายุ) 51

Agree

    Agree - hĕn-dûai (เห็นด้วย) 55

    Agree, yes - châi (ใช่) 65

Aids to Memory

    Aids to Memory I 26

    Aids to Memory II 29

Aim - fài (ใฝ่) 141

Aiyarah (ไอยารา) - name of the elephant 64, 138

Àksɔ̆ɔn (อักษร) - consonant 9

All

    All - táng (ทั้ง) 31

    All - táng-mòt (ทั้งหมด) 77

    All, whole, entire - sàp (สรรพ) 141

Almost dry - màat (หมาด) 34

Also - gɔ̂ (ก็) 37

Amuse, have fun, play - lêen (เล่น) 117

An (อัน) - classifier for small object and things in general 144

And - lɛ́ (และ) 37, 69, 75, 79, 117

Ang-grit (อังกฤษ) - English 50, 131

Angry - gròot (โกรธ) 142, 156

An-năi (อันไหน) - which 94

Any - dai (ใด) 140

Apache (อาปาชี) - name of the horse 110, 139

Appearance - mâat (มาด) 34

April - mee-săa-yon (เมษายน) 102

À-rai (อะไร) - what 46, 48, 50, 116, 154

Are you well - kun sà-baai dii măi (คุณสบายดีไหม) 153

Armies - gɔɔng-táp (กองทัพ) 77

Arrange, prepare - jàt (จัด) 28

Arrive, reach - tŭng (ถึง) 89

Arrogant - húk hə̆əm (ฮึกเหิม) 133

Arrow - sɔ̆ɔn (ศร) 32

À-rɔ̀ɔi

    À-rɔ̀ɔi (อร่อย) - delicious 157

    À-rɔ̀ɔi mâak (อร่อยมาก) - very delicious 106, 157

Ashara (อาซารา) - name of the snake 58, 138

Ask - tăam (ถาม) 51, 89, 155

At

    At (location), straight - dtrong (ตรง) 142

    At 2 pm - bàai sɔ̆ɔng moong dtrong (บ่าย 2 โมงตรง) 61

    At that time - ná wee-laa-nán (ณ เวลานั้น) 83

August - sĭng-hăa-kom (สิงหาคม) 102

B

Bàai sɔ̆ɔng moong dtrong (บ่าย 2 โมงตรง) - at 2 pm 60

Baan (บาน) - classifier for windows, doors, picture frames, mirrors 144

Bâan (บ้าน) - house, home 52, 97

Bàat (บาด) - cut 17, 84

Bad - leeo (เลว) 117, 156

Bag - tŭng (ถุง) 88

Bai

    Bai (ใบ) - classifier for empty glasses 144

    Bai (ใบ) - leaf 94, 140

    Bai níi (ใบนี้) - this leaf 96

Bâi (ใบ้) - mute, dumb 140

Bai-mái (ใบไม้) - leaf 97

Bake - òp (อบ) 157

Bangkok - Grung-têep-má-hăa-ná-kɔɔn (กรุงเทพมหานคร) 140

Ban-jù (บรรจุ) - load, fill 141

Banyan Tree - sai (ไทร) 143

Bao (เบา) - light (weight) 156

Barbeque, grill, roast - yâang (ย่าง) 157

Bathroom - hɔ̂ɔng nám (ห้องน้ำ) 24

Be careful - rá-wang (ระวัง) 129

Be somewhere, locate - yùu (อยู่) 131

Beautiful - sŭai (สวย) 119, 156

Because - prɔ́-wâa (เพราะว่า) 67

Bedroom - hɔ̂ɔng nɔɔn (ห้องนอน) 24

Bee - pûng (ผึ้ง) 100

Beef - núua (เนื้อ) 157

Been (เบน) - turn away 37

L

P

Pàan (ผ่าน) – cross, pass 101

Paan (พาน) - tray 16, 105

Pâap (ภาพ) – picture, drawing 109

Paa-săa (ภาษา) – language, speech, words 109

Package - hɔ̀ɔ (ห่อ) 20

Pàd Thai (ผัดไทย) - noodles Thai style 157

Pain - jèp (เจ็บ) 70

Pák (พัก) - rest 70

Pan-rá-yaa (ภรรยา) - wife 60

Papaya salad - sôm-dtam (ส้มตำ) 157

Parade - dəən kà-buan (เดินขบวน) 63

Parcel - hɔ̀ɔ (ห่อ) 20

Party - ngaan-líiang (งานเลี้ยง) 103

Pass - pàan (ผ่าน) 101

Pàt (ผัด) - fry 157

Path - mák (มรรค) 141

Pavilion/Tent - săa-laa (ศาลา) 120

Pá-yaa-baan (พยาบาล) - nurse 158

Pedestal - tăan (ฐาน) 76

Pen - bpàak-gaa (ปากกา) 22

Perform - bpà-dti-bàt (ปฏิบัติ) 75

Perhaps - àat (อาจ) 53

Permit - hâi (ให้) 141

Person

    Person - kon (คน) 54

    Person - pûu (ผู้) 81

Pèt (เผ็ด) - spicy 157

Pèt mâak (เผ็ดมาก) - very spicy 157

Phoebe (ฟีบี้) - one of the party bee's 105

Picture, drawing - pâap (ภาพ) 109

Pĭi

    Pĭi (พี่) - older sibling 56, 105

    Pĭi-chaai (พี่ชาย) - older brother 61

    Pĭi-nɔ́ɔng (พี่น้อง) - relative 61

    Pĭi-săao (พี่สาว) - older sister 61

Pik-kù (ภิกขุ) - bhikkus, ordained monks 94

Pilot - nák-bin (นักบิน) 158

Pineapple - sàp-bpà-rót (สับปะรด) 158

Pink - sĭi chom-puu (สีชมพู) 156

Pìt (ผิด) – wrong, incorrect 101

Place - waang (วาง) 16

Plàk (ผลัก) - push, shove 142, 155

Plank, sheet - pɛ̀ɛn (แผ่น) 101

Plate - jaan (จาน) 60

Play, have fun, amuse - lêen (เล่น) 117, 155

Please

    Please - gà-rú-naa (กรุณา) 153

    Please repeat that - gà-rú-naa pûut ìik tii (กรุณาพูดอีกที) 154

    Please speak slowly - gà-rú-naa pûut cháa cháa nɔ̀ɔi (กรุณาพูดช้า ๆ หน่อย) 154

Plík (พลิก) - turn over 142

Poem, poetry - kloong (โคลง) 142

Policeman - dtam-rùat (ตำรวจ) 158

Pollo (พอลโล่) - name of the egg 49, 138

Pŏm

    Pŏm (ผม) - I, me (male) 154

    Pŏm bpen kon ang-grìt (ผมเป็นคนอังกฤษ) - I am English 51

    Pŏm bpen kon sòot (ผมเป็นคนโสด) - I am single 23

    Pŏm bpen nák-riian (ผมเป็นนักเรียน) - I am a student 23

    Pŏm chนน... (ผมชื่อ...) - my name is (male) 153

    Pŏm dนนm biia lɛ́ɛo (ผมดื่มเบียร์แล้ว) - I drank beer already 21

    Pŏm gam-lang dนนm biia (ผมกำลังดื่มเบียร์) - I am drinking beer 21

    Pŏm hĭo (ผมหิว) - I am hungry 22

    Pŏm jà dนนm biia (ผมจะดื่มเบียร์) - I will drink beer 21

    Pŏm mâi mii (ผมไม่มี) - I don't have one 154

    Pŏm pûut tai mâi dâi (ผมพูดไทยไม่ได้) - I don't speak Thai 154

    Pŏm sà-baai dii (ผมสบายดี) - I am well 48, 153

    Pŏm yùu tîi nîi (ผมอยู่ที่นี่) - I am over here 22

    Pŏm... mâi dâi (ผม...ไม่ได้) - I cannot... 52

Pŏn-lá-mái (ผลไม้) - fruit 38

Poor - jon (จน) 156

Póp (พบ) - meet, find 97, 155

Pork - mŭu (หมู) 157

Position - tăa-ná (ฐานะ) 77

Postman - bù-rùt-bprai-sà-nii (บุรุษไปรษณีย์) 158

Pót-jà-naa-nú-grom (พจนานุกรม) - dictionary 38

Prá (พระ) - Buddha image or statue 142

Precinct - mon-ton (มณฑล) 79

Prepare, arrange - jàt (จัด) 28

Prík (พริก) - chilli 157

Problem - bpan-hăa (ปัญหา) 67

Property - sáp (ทรัพย์) 143

Protect, defend - bpòk-bpɔ̂ɔng (ปกป้อง) 73

Prûng-nii (พรุ่งนี้) - tomorrow 74, 98

Prɔ́-wâa (เพราะว่า) - because 66

Prɔ́ɔm (พร้อม) - ready 56

Pŭa (ผัว) - husband (informal) 61

Pûak

    Pûak (พวก) - more than one 155

    Pûak-kăo (พวกเขา) - they 46, 90, 100, 102, 155

    Pûak-rao (พวกเรา) - us, we 46, 78, 155

Pull - dนng (ดึง) 69, 113, 155

Purple - sĭi mûang (สีม่วง) 156

Push - plàk (ผลัก) 142, 155

Put

    Put (down), place - waang (วาง) 16, 155

    Put in, add - sài (ใส่) 125, 140

Pút-saa (พุทรา) - type of fruit 143

T

Y

Z

4112845R00101

Printed in Great Britain
by Amazon.co.uk, Ltd.,
Marston Gate.